THE ELASTIC ENTERPRISE:

The new manifesto for business revolution

by

Nicholas Vitalari and Haydn Shaughnessy

TELEMACHUS PRESS

This is a work of nonfiction. The opinions and information expressed are solely those of the authors. No warranties, either expressed or implied, are provided by the authors or the publisher.

The Elastic Enterprise: The new manifesto for business revolution

The publisher does not have any control over and does not assume any responsibility for author or third-party websites or their content.

Cover Designed by Jen Bigora

Cover Art by Joseph Vitalari

Published by Telemachus Press, LLC

http://www.telemachuspress.com

Visit the author website:
http://www.theelasticenterprise.com

ISBN: 978-0-9852-4983-0 (eBook)
ISBN: 978-1-938135-33-0 (ePub)
ISBN: 978-1-938135-34-7 (Paperback)

Library of Congress Control Number: 2012936841

Version 2012.09.19

TO OUR READERS

In the spirit of The Elastic Enterprise, this book is just the beginning. We have set up a website at www.theelasticenterprise.com so that we can expand on the issues we address in the book. The Elastic Enterprise contains a number of novel concepts for explaining wealth creation and competitive success so on the website we'll dive deeper into those as well as post some of our background research papers. You are very welcome to join the debate.

Our production process for the book uses elastic concepts too. We originally published the book in electronic format and took into account the feedback of readers to produce the print version. Along the way we've worked with a growing business ecosystem of publishers, distributors, artists and reviewers that make up the new scene in electronic and print publishing.

Being elastic is a mission. The discussions and development of ideas will continue, so you are not buying a book, you are buying into an evolving project to redefine the way we work and how we create wealth and competitiveness. Please join us on a regular basis for the latest updates on "being elastic" in your company, your work and your career at:

www.theelasticenterprise.com

We welcome any questions, comments or inquiries:

All the best and much success in your work.

Nick Vitalari   Haydn Shaughnessy

TABLE OF CONTENTS

PREFACE

Some time ago we asked the CEO of a Fortune 500 company what kept him awake at night. His answer was: "I just don't know how much more energy I can spend bringing my 19th century organization into the 21st."

Perhaps his employees and partners were asking the same question.

His answer conjured up an image of a claptrap vehicle trundling along unmade country roads while his peers drive their sleek cars on the highway.

The image stuck with us when we began writing up the results of our research1 into companies that have become stellar performers during the worst recession on record.

Policy makers, executives, employees, small businesses around the world are asking how can we create a different kind of engine for growth? What's next?

This book investigates what the pioneers are doing differently and what they can teach us about doing business in a radically new way.

We believe the techniques that the best performers have invented will spur a new era of economic growth and that their lessons are applicable to companies of all sizes.

A new manifesto for business revolution is emerging.

The book is not about the superficial aspects of a company's marketing or its brand.

It spells out a small number of fundamentals, five simple dynamics that all enterprises can apply to improve their competitiveness, grow without incurring heavy costs of scale and rediscover the pleasure of being at work.

But it is also about a new model for creating societal wealth.

Pioneer companies have uncovered new ways to scale their businesses. They have broken the mold set over two hundred years ago by Scottish philosopher and economist Adam Smith.

We call these companies *elastic enterprises.*

And we want to help you understand how you can master the same skills that these pioneers have developed.

In particular we will explain how they manage to integrate many strands of change into one coherent strategy. And why their employees, customers, partners and analysts seem to adore it.

We don't want to waste your time with a theory about business or management.

While other companies were laying staff off, these were hiring and creating opportunity for vast ecosystems of creative people. We noticed these companies were not just good for employment opportunities; they were creating new markets as well.

We are talking here about real change, along many dimensions, baked into one coherent model for how business should be done

More than that, though, it is a model that can supply answers to the questions people are raising about society in general and our broader economic model. Elastic enterprises represent a new model for creating societal wealth, a new way of working together.

After the turmoil of the past five years people are asking is our way of doing things bankrupt? Have our institutions ground to a halt?

Or, on a more optimistic note, they're asking what's next?

We will answer those questions in this book. Here are some more you might be asking.

1. Is it feasible to build a successful growth strategy for an unpredictable future?
2. How can innovation really transform a company instead of wasting more management time on catch-up?
3. What structures and mechanisms will exploit the power of an instantaneously connected world, which ones will leave you high and dry?
4. How should enterprises understand and meet the needs of the changing global customer base?
5. What is the new role of the leader?
6. What is the best way to reach beyond a company's core competency?
7. How do you give your enterprise the passion and belief of a movement?

Our shorthand answer to these pressing questions is to become an elastic enterprise. In the shortest possible space we will explain what that means and the difference it makes to executives, employees, partners and customers.

---

[1] In preparing the book we have researched the practices and leadership styles of over 80 companies that were adopting open, elastic strategies. We compiled a checklist of elasticity to gauge their level or maturity on the path towards becoming a different type of enterprise. We interviewed over two hundred executives in various companies about their innovation strategies, new market developments, and their frustrations and successes. In writing the book we have not quoted directly from any of the executives we have talked to and have relied for the most part on sources that are available in the public domain in order to protect any confidences that have been shared with us.

CHAPTER 1
INNOVATION OR TRANSFORMATION?

The Strange Case of Companies that Grow in Recession

From 2007 and the onset of recession a small group of companies began enjoying exceptional sales and profit growth, companies like Apple and Amazon.com to name the most obvious. They didn't just grow. They didn't just enjoy their most successful years. The best of them began performing like no other company before.

At the same time, another group of companies headed for the bottom.

Companies such as Nokia, who prior to 2009 enjoyed a totally dominant position in the mobile phone industry, mobile e-mail pioneer RIM, telecoms infrastructure leader Cisco, electronics giant Sony, a household name with a dazzling record of product innovation, all were distinctive companies that were suddenly struggling to survive.

How come?

We believe that the answer is simple and exciting. A new type of enterprise emerged in the first decade of the 21st century and its processes and techniques are repeatable and replicable by companies with ambition.

We call this new type of company an *elastic enterprise.*

Elastic enterprises represent a new generation of competitive strategy and new operating processes that together form a remarkable response to changing economic conditions.

Elastic enterprises are a new, more dynamic, and more inclusive approach to wealth creation.

What allowed companies like Apple and Amazon to succeed, while their competitors failed, is the subject of this book.

But Apple and Amazon are by no means alone. Nor is this story simply about high-tech companies.

The dimensions of the new business revolution go broad and deep and the lessons can be applied across many industries and many different types of businesses. Among the exponents that deserve a special mention are UK newspaper The Guardian, Korean giant Next Human Network, travel platform Expedia, even the formerly staid New York Times.

Nor, clearly, is this simply an American success story.

While the revolution may have begun in the U.S. and some of the most dramatic examples of wealth creation are seen in Apple and Amazon, they represent only the first chapter of the story.

We see elastic enterprises emerging in traditional industries as well as emerging economies. And we see a number of long-lived companies, like GE and Caterpillar that are adding elastic elements to their businesses.

Markers of Elasticity

The most obvious character of elastic enterprises is that, first, they've proved themselves to be successful in the bad times.

But secondly and significantly they are also operating on a new scale, typically with many thousands of business partners.

They are also stepping effortlessly from their core businesses into adjacent businesses, from computing hardware into service platforms and then into mobile devices and apps as Apple did with iTunes and iPhone. Or with Amazon—from books to a broad base of retail products and then into Cloud infrastructure and services.

In other industries, GE Aviation has added a sophisticated business platform to collect inflight engine data for its aircraft engine business, and then formed a global aircraft maintenance business with many global partners. Today they have mobile apps, new service models, sophisticated alliances with avionics manufacturers and cooperative arrangements with other aircraft engine manufacturers. Such developments have propagated to other GE businesses.

The same progression can be seen at companies like Deere and Caterpillar, as they expand their businesses globally.

Google too, as you would expect, exhibits similar traits.

The best of these companies are taking the most difficult strategies in business and executing with apparent ease while their peers are struggling to hold onto market share with an outdated operating model.

The reasons for their success are undoubtedly rooted in technological advance, in mobility and Cloud, as well as the vast interconnections of the Internet. But in a sense those are givens, infrastructure that every company has access to. The true leaders and pioneers are doing something else that gives them exceptional market advantages.

While their peers might be focused on innovation or agility, these companies are transformative. They are changing the way business is done.

We call the collection of strategies and operating principles that create this new level of success *the elastic enterprise* to distinguish it from other operating models, and to highlight the fact that elasticity is not really about innovation or agility.

If success only relied on innovation, Sony would still be a dominant force in consumer electronics. And if agility was the only necessary requirement of the modern age then Nokia, with its multiple, annual product releases would still be the dominant force in smartphones.

It is essential that we learn from the elastic enterprise's success. Your company should aspire not just to emulate an Apple or an

Amazon but more importantly to embrace a highly effective new operating model.

We want to describe the new operating model for you in this book.

To understand it we will introduce a series of new concepts. They're simple but powerful.

The key concepts we will use are:

1. Radical adjacency
2. Mass differentiation
3. The new scale economics
4. Sapient leadership
5. Active strategy
6. The five dynamics of the elastic enterprise

Radical adjacency. Adjacency moves are notoriously difficult for companies to make. Elastic enterprises are showing it is possible to make radical adjacency moves, moves into geographical markets or new product areas that do not reflect a company's core competency. In fact radical adjacency *redefines* core competency (more of which later). It means stepping outside the core and operating in new markets with assurance and ease. Elastic enterprise leaders typically implement radical adjacency strategies.

Mass differentiation. Markets can no longer be segmented on traditional demographic lines. In a new global economy companies must *elicit* market segments from data and customer interaction. Customers are defining their own needs and their own market reference groups.

In essence the long tail is becoming the market. That means companies must be capable of offering far more diversity in their product categories. Expedia, for example, revamped its affiliate program in order to empower affiliates to frame product offerings to their hyper-local, and hyper-niche markets. Instead of one Expedia there were suddenly dozens of new hyper-local, content rich travel offerings in the market. This is typical of an elastic enterprise, creating mass differentiation, and securing greater customer loyalty through partners.

The new scale economics. Mass differentiation is part of a new economics of scale. Traditional scale economics were built by growing a company's internal resources, through capital investment and hiring. Today scale takes place through ecosystems of freely collaborating third parties.

Sapient leadership. Because growth takes place through business ecosystems, those free floating collaborations of independent businesses and creative people, leadership can no longer be commanding and demanding.

Both Apple and Amazon have had to concede ground to their ecosystems and their businesses have benefited immeasurably from it.

We call the new leadership sapient because we want to convey a new capability. That is the ability to appear, to an independent ecosystem, as a leader operating on behalf of the mutual interests of the group.

Sapient leaders are constantly in the eye of their peers, are judged by their peers daily, and their peers are running smart, educated, savvy businesses. The relationship matters critically to success. The leader has to be perceived by peers as wise.

Active strategy. To serve markets that experience mass differentiation, strategy has to be both continuous (as distinct from episodic) and active—in pursuit of new opportunities that emerge even in real-time.

Active strategy is also defined by the presence of active strategic portfolio management, a continuous creation of new strategic options, and knowing when to execute or to hold back. Active strategy requires a significant change in the mindset of the senior executive team and the strategy execution process.

The five dynamics of the new operating model. Finally we will talk about five dynamics of the elastic enterprise. These are business platforms (iTunes for example), business ecosystems, which we already mentioned, universal connectors (technologies that facilitate friction free commerce through automated online interactions, for example RSS feeds and application programming interfaces), Cloud computing (the new friction free IT infrastructure), and of course sapient leadership.

These new capabilities are being driven by global change and by specific technological advances. The most important are mobility and data. Although we allude to these throughout the book, we have chosen not to make this a book about mobility or data. It is specifically about how the capabilities of the elastic enterprise position businesses to exploit the new technological and global landscape of business.

It is about the transformational response to dramatically changing conditions, brought to you by highly effective business leaders.

The Elastic Enterprise
Elastic enterprises are forging the operating principles that transition us to a new form of wealth creation. They operate in a profoundly different way from companies that are still using the industrial-service model of operating.

We became interested in these organizations because of their competitiveness and performance.

Over a three year period we studied over 80 such organizations. Not all of them by any means are elastic but most are on their way to this new form of wealth generation.

Among the companies we studied are Apple, Spanish bank BBVA, Boeing, Walmart, The Guardian, Marriott, USAA, CNN, Disney, Forbes, Ford, BMW, GE, PayPal, Salesforce, Amazon, YUM! Brands, Starbucks, Netflix, Thomson Reuters, Lenovo, Kaiser Permanente, Expedia, the New York Times, Caterpillar, FedEx, Google, Amex, MasterCard, and SWIFT.

The best of these didn't just grow. They didn't just begin to enjoy their best ever years. More significantly, they began performing like no other company before them.

Apple exemplifies that success more than any other company and provides us with a working definition of the elastic enterprise:

The Elastic Enterprise involves a whole new approach to scaling a business, which we've described through five interlocking dynamics.

However, its true defining characteristic is the ability to grow at an unprecedented rate, relative to the **cost** of scale (the new scale economics).

Its main avenues of growth are:

Radical adjacency, which takes companies into entirely new markets, and redefines core competency around the five dynamics, and rapidly scaled, low friction, human interaction, and automated contractual relationships that allow new business partnerships to form instantly.

The guiding objective for senior executives in the new era should be: to seek scale without incurring the disproportionate overhead that currently accompanies growth, and to enjoy a flexibility of maneuver through radical adjacency that has not previously been possible at scale.

These qualities are visible in the case of Apple and Amazon but also in less celebrated cases such as USAA, Forbes, and Expedia.

There is no getting away from it, however, Apple is the most astounding implementation of elastic principles

Apple's revenues in the third quarter of its 2010–2011 fiscal year were up 82% and profits were up 125%. This would be a supreme achievement at any time but the summer of 2011 was not a holiday period, where sales tend to be strong. And the economy still teetered on the edge of recession.

Apple was not just succeeding wildly. On the way to record profits, Steve Jobs' team had created monumental disruption in a product category (smartphones) that the company had inhabited for a total of only four years. Shortly after entering smartphones, Apple created a new product category (tablets) single handedly with the launch of the iPad.

This was unusual success heaped on top of astonishing corporate performance.

Of course Apple has a history of introducing disruptive products but its original disruption, in desktop computing, was thirty years earlier when Apple was founded. Never in its history has Apple sidestepped the opposition so frequently and so effectively as the past five years.

Crucially, on this occasion it did so by creating partnerships, at huge scale, through the App Store, illustrating for the first time how a new kind of scale economics could drive business.

Amazon.com is a parallel case.

With the launch of its Kindle e-book reader, Amazon suddenly converted itself into a device company, a move that would normally spell chaos.

Amazon.com had previously pioneered what became known as "platform as a service" and "cloud computing," a revolution in how companies source their IT needs.

With these disruptive radical adjacencies, like Apple, Amazon opened new horizons for itself during a severe recession by doing what companies should not do—move into adjacent markets with entirely new products.

From early 2008 to mid-2011, Amazon roughly tripled top line revenues.

In 2010/2011, alone, Amazon's revenues from its consumer electronics business surged 69% during an extremely weak recovery from recession.

The remarkable feature of Amazon growth was that its profits briefly fell during the period, yet its share price rose. Barron's called it a "religion stock," one you believe in or you don't.

The highly conservative forces of Wall Street, the market makers, the dealmakers, the analysts and the observers voted a big yes to Amazon.com's convention-breaking moves. Stock market seers—normally so conservative when it comes to disruption—love it.

But let's be clear about what they love. We live in an age of hyperinnovation where every company is urged to innovate in some form or another.

Amazon is not just innovating. If it were only innovating, it would not be that different from its peers. Wall Street analysts are applauding transformational strategies, strategies that transform the way business is done. That is Amazon's achievement, and it is Apple's too.

Markets typically do not like disruptive change. They abhor maverick leaders. Their endorsement of Amazon.com and their love affair with Apple suggests something profoundly different is going on—a change recognized by both pioneer leaders and market analysts.

Apple, a decade back, was a wasted power in niche computing, selling its OS-leading products to universities and graphic designers.

Apple began in 2001 to build its iTunes business platform. They diversified their product base with successive introductions of the iPod, and simultaneously moved aggressively into the music industry.

By 2007, Apple began the reinvention of mobile telephony, creating a whole new way of packaging and marketing software (the app), one that became so successful that sales of iPhone and iPad apps are metered in the billions.

Apple is in some sense unique, you might argue. There was only one Steve Jobs. And its position in computing was always as the outsider loved by millions. Arguably it could have sprung a surprise on the market at any time by drawing on the genius of Jobs and designer Jonathan Ive. But what Apple did was much more than a left-field innovation.

We need to see in Apple an example of what is possible, having established a high performance business platform (in iTunes) and a strong ecosystem. These new tools mean that they are now able to make radical adjacency moves at will. They can act like predators and select from their strategic options portfolio, where and when they will strike next, not always successfully but successfully enough to be the single most admired company in the world.

Apple builds its success through its platform and ecosystem as well as its products.

But Apple itself is a great emulator of good examples.

In building out its platform (the business platform is a key dynamic of the elastic enterprise), Apple undoubtedly learned from the internal supply chain platform of Walmart and the product customization platform of Dell, two platform and global manufacturing pioneers.

What Apple also showed us with iTunes and the App Store is that marketing is no longer about demographics, the A, B, C1, C2 or income-based segmentation that dominated during the era of mass marketing.

Apple's success reflects a change in the way markets are structured.

Jobs did not set out to sell its apps to a demographic. He did something entirely unconventional and rule breaking.

Whereas in the past, a company's supply chain, the people who contribute to its products, were kept out back, Apple put its app developers out front, next to the customer, and the two began to mix. Through the ecosystem they created a flow of ideas, products and consumer demand. The ecosystem strategy had been used before, for example by Microsoft with its Value-Added Resellers' network. But never before in a set of open relationships in consumer markets.

Free-flowing ecosystems of producers and consumers are the new route to market segmentation, backed by advanced data analytics that let vendors aggregate and interpret buyer behavior on the fly. Flow has replaced structure.

With the iPhone Apple also created a highly componentized world that in effect makes you, the consumer, a market of 1. The relationship between a cornerstone company in an ecosystem and the consumer is itself in transition. Consumers can now self-select the communities or segments they belong to.

Only you have precisely the collection of Apps, videos and songs that sits on your phone.

Ok, so in a market of millions somebody somewhere will have duplicated your precise collection of apps, videos and songs.

But the significant change is that the customer now defines herself in this market.

Apple did not create a dozen apps and market them to you, nor try to predict all of the apps you might want. It created a platform where hundreds of thousands of developers created hundreds of thousands of options for you.

You, the market of 1, created the product mix. As you choose more apps you define the functionality and value of the product in an open-ended process of discovery that keeps pace with your needs.

This is what we mean by mass differentiation. Mass differentiation is different from mass customization.

Mass customization allows customers to adapt a mass produced product. What we are seeing in mass differentiation is a new generation of strategies that allow companies to serve many thousands of micro-markets.

That is what Apple has done with its App Store, what Google is attempting with its productivity apps marketplace, and what newspapers like The Guardian want to do with their open innovation project.

In the early days of social media the big conundrum for marketers was how to communicate with customers online. Companies did not communicate. They outsourced that to call centers. Suddenly customer activity online drew them back into personal relationships.

Mass differentiation is increasing that pressure to understand markets and to relate to customers at the most granular level.

Companies as disparate as Boeing with its new Airplane Health Management, Kaiser Permanente with its HealthConnect program, Expedia and its new affiliate programs, CNN with its next generation iReport, Forbes with its giant new blogging platform, BMW with its new mobility fund, Formula 1 engineers McLaren's new health analytics service, are all attempting this reinvention, going beyond steady state innovations to a new way of business, serving micro-markets for the first time. To do that they are adopting the new elastic enterprise operating system.

And already you've seen the idea of a business platform and a business ecosystem in action (the Apple, Google, Guardian, or Amazon developer community and their new relationship with customers).

Active strategy (see Chapter 6), in contrast to traditional business strategy is a consequence of these innovations. When you are addressing globally differentiated markets, strategy can no longer be episodic, annual or even bi-annual. It has to be continuous and a part of the daily diet.

The New Scale Economics

So is elasticity really about innovation or about something entirely new?

Our belief is that innovation, as practiced today, is primarily about method—how to create a new product, or service, or improve an existing one.

That doesn't begin to describe what is taking place in elastic enterprises.

Today we live on an amped up, instantaneously connected planet. Anyone—any corporation, any government or any group—can immediately communicate and engage in complex transactions with anyone, and with the advent of M2M (Machine to Machine) commerce, anything on the planet at any time. This new reality connects people with information, ideas and knowledge without regard to boundaries.

Elastic enterprises take advantage of an instantaneously connected world to manage people and resources in new ways, to scale in ways not possible in a 20th Century enterprise and to broaden the strategic vision of enterprise wealth creation.

One of the main transformations that the elastic enterprise brings then is a new form of scale. Rapid scale at low risk and low cost, infused with participation from wholly new groups of economic actors that are now being called business ecosystems.

This transformation is as important as the one Adam Smith noted 235 years ago when he saw nail makers break their tasks down into more specialized skill components.

Alongside the benefits of the division of labor, we can now have a new set of principles for how human organization can function at a super-effective level.

Large non-elastic organizations create profound dis-economies. Scale has come to equate with sclerosis because the costs associated with organizing more and more people scale more quickly than the additional wealth those people create.

Implicit in the elastic enterprise is something absolutely crucial to the new way of business—a much cheaper way of organizing people and a more efficient way of allocating resources.

We are inventing mechanisms that prioritize a new, highly scaled form of *self*-organization, along with new principles that govern the interchange of value between economic actors.

Pioneers of elastic business models are eliminating or at least radically reducing the old organizational overhead.

- There is no longer a fixed imperative to think of expansion in terms of new hires

- There is no need to scale infrastructure through capital expenditures (CAPX) now that we are growing a Cloud infrastructure.

- There is no need for a complex Value Added Resellers (VAR), Independent Software Vendors (ISV) or partnership model as hierarchical partnerships are replaced by business ecosystems.

- Legal partnerships are giving way to universally applicable program enrollment, for example in developer communities.

These strategies embrace new economic actors, such as the creative industries (Forbes, YouTube, The Guardian), and they embrace existing economic actors like developers (Apple, Google, Amazon) in new ways.

The new economic actors are not necessarily employees or partners. They are something in between. In fact the elastic enterprise transforms our notion of what the primary economic relationships are and can be.

It is estimated that Apple has between 100,000 and 300,000 developers working on its behalf—at their own risk. By the way, the estimates depend on whether you count who has signed up on the developer network in its lifetime (over a million) or only those that program in the native iOS programming language, Objective-C.

Suffice it to say, it's a big number regardless of the technical details. Google also has a relatively large group of global developers for its Android OS and content creators for it YouTube ecosystem. Amazon has a growing base of programmers and technologists conversant with their Amazon Web Services Cloud ecosystem.

Forbes has 800 new content contributors on an incentive, rather than salaried, basis. CNN has a relationship with thousands of content creators that they do not pay. All interact with customers. Giving suppliers direct access to customers would have been anathema in the old days of doing business.

Of course this entails new relationship-building skills.

The new economic actors have to be treated well, without being pandered to. They are not just suppliers; they are a mediator of relationships with customers, and sales, a funnel for important market data, and a mechanism to serve those all-important-markets.

They are not just cheap sources of wealth production.

While many in number, they do not need a supervisory hierarchy.

Better than that, they are often impassioned sources of labor, people with real commitment to their roles and their creativity, who are capable of seeking out new ways of creating value.

They present the cornerstone enterprise with a mechanism to scale business rapidly into areas where it does not have indigenous insight and skills.

This then is not just about labor flexibility.

The new economic relationships are the basis on which radical adjacency moves are built.

And they are what allow large cornerstone enterprise like Apple to create and respond to mass differentiation.

The new scale economics are a revolution and are available to any company that depends on consumer markets, either directly or through partnerships and wants to do business in a radically new way. The challenge for many companies, though, is that they are stuck in traditional structures and processes that stand in the way of transformation.

To understand it properly, to articulate the chief characteristics of the elastic enterprise, it is important to put it in the context of change in the global economy.

The New Phase of Globalization and Mass Differentiation

The corollary of scale is that elastic organizations can and do serve micro-markets. Unlike the past, they are not scaling to serve mass markets, through mass media communications. Their operating principles allow them to grow through mass differentiation. This is so profound that we have yet to grasp its full implications.

The changing nature of global business creates an incessant demand for enterprise *elasticity*. *Global business is digital and physical—no longer one or the other. Global business is hyper competitive, fuelled by new, fast developing markets and production centers like China.*

And global business is a major source of enterprise growth. To be successful in this environment requires an enterprise to have global information and global relationship building capabilities. But ironically that global market is also fragmenting at the consumer level into many thousands of micro-markets or hyper-channels. And it is happening fast, across the globe.

As the number of users on the Internet approaches two billion or roughly 30% of the world's total population, the opportunity, complexity and the competitive landscape for business expands dramatically.[1] For the first time the most significant change is not taking place in the advanced markets.

During the period 2000 to 2010, the number of Internet users grew at approximately 445%, with Africa leading the way at 2,357%, followed by the Middle East at 1,825% and Latin America at 1,033%, despite two global recessions during this period.

When considered in absolute terms, the number of users on the Internet is led by Asia at 825.1 million, Europe at 475.1 million, followed by North America at 266.2 million with the remaining approximately 600 million distributed across other geographies. Much of this growth has been aided, particularly in developing countries, by the emergence of low-cost mobile devices and infrastructure as the primary form of information technology, bringing more and more people into the web of scaled interaction.

Not only is this a globally interconnected world, outside the developed economies, a new middle class is emerging with unprecedented speed.

In India, according to the McKinsey Global Institute,[2] the "average household income will triple over the next two decades and it will become the world's 5th-largest consumer economy by 2025, up from 12th now."

That's on top of a decade where extreme poverty has been eradicated in many parts of the subcontinent. India's middle class will grow from 50 million in 2010 to 585 million in 2025, reflecting a huge expansion of spending power.

If that sounds dramatic then consider this too: The World Bank estimates that the global middle class is likely to grow from 430 million in 2000 to 1.15 billion in 2030 and what we now think of as developing economies will contribute over 93% of the global middle class, China alone contributing 52%.

The "scale-value" of products increases also, becoming more dynamic and perhaps even unpredictable. What one person loves can become a phenomenon that millions love in a matter minutes or days. Product launches have become globally shared events accompanied by unprecedented adoption and participation rates.

Indigenous business communities and related experience are also growing globally. For the last eight years, The World Bank has been tracking business regulations in 183 countries to understand the ease of doing business in various regions, nations and cities. The latest study, *Doing Business 2011: Making a Difference for Entrepreneurs*, reported that from 2005 to 2010, the "doing business score" has advanced significantly in 85% of the nations studied. Other studies of global economic growth[3] point to similar conclusions.

Although not uniformly distributed, most areas of the world are embarking on global growth. The prognosis for overall improvement in income levels in developing countries and the corresponding increase in indigent purchasing power is positive.

Taken together, these global economic factors create favorable conditions for the emergence of the elastic enterprise based around business platforms, business ecosystems, universal connectors, cloud infrastructure and new leadership.

With diverse and distant global markets, companies can attract and delight customers anywhere, any time. Yet if business models don't change then the time and cost of capturing these markets might make them effectively inaccessible. Done the right way companies will be able to scale up their operations while simultaneously managing smaller markets that may, in the past, have had real diseconomies of scale.[4]

In fact, one of the underlying market conditions is a new degree of market heterogeneity that is both geographic and extends beyond geography.

As well as having to serve many diverse markets around the world, companies must also appeal to a new level of intra-market differentiation. People are demanding even more differentiated lifestyles, and are able to source "differentness" via the web.

Companies need to think in terms of more product variety and more products that meet a wider array of customer needs.

This is true for all products in a complex world of diverse global demands.

Pharmaceuticals are a perfect example of the need for mass differentiation and the cost of not building up a platform for delivering it.

All prescription drugs have to go through three phases of clinical trial before approval.

In the case of cancer treatment, many trials show surprisingly good results for a small portion of the trial population. However, if, for example, three people from a population of 40 enjoy spectacular outcomes for a trial medicine, the trial is considered a spectacular failure. No drug would progress from here to approval.

Consider though that those three people might represent some form of cure for people like them.

The other thirty-seven people clearly need another form of treatment. The three however represent a perfect case of mass differentiation—added to all the people of that type globally, the trial medicine might well be a breakthrough.

Our current conception of mass markets forces us to reject that drug. We perceive only one type of patient. We treat the three as flukes.

In a world of massive computational power, the consequence of this finding should be to identify more people like the three rather than to reject the drug.

If that were to happen, it might mean that a population of 40 people needs 15 types of treatment, i.e., mass differentiation.

However, our mass production-era sensibilities prevent us from seeing the value of mass differentiation because we are programmed to drive towards a one-size-fits-all formula for most products.

Businesses must forge new business models and modes of operation that can reach a growing, diversifying and developing world population of customers. They have to move beyond old classifications—old notions of customer income groups or class divisions—to serve a market of mass differentiation.

They must create flexibility that moves the focal point of competitiveness away from employed labor towards people with the aspiration to own and operate their own companies or with the talent to solve customer problems, often in micro-markets.

In the process, they must create a new foundation that incorporates the creativity and innovation of a globally interconnected community.

And they must find ways to operate outside the business cycle, with a new kind of elasticity that is not based on hire and fire but is more self-regulating and dependent on the laws and dependencies of self-sustaining ecosystems.

These are the conditions that we believe are fast emerging around us. The elastic enterprise helps leaders to exploit markets more effectively because those leaders recognize the heterogeneous nature of markets and the similarities of middle class aspirations.

To use a term first coined eight years ago, they see that the long tail is now the main market and that means the market is comprised of many thousands of niches large enough for global organizations to exploit.

We are going to argue that the elastic enterprise is an organic response to those market conditions.

Beyond Innovation: Transformation and the Leap to The Elastic Enterprise

The mantra of the past decade has been *innovation*. A widespread expectation, or hope, has been that innovation will bring companies closer to aligning with the demands of a new economic environment.

The elastic enterprise is clearly about innovation but it is an important step beyond it too. We are at a point in the development of enterprises where companies must transform in order to innovate at the level of creativity and execution they need in order to be competitive.

The problem we identify with innovation, as we said earlier, is that, by and large, most writers on the topic are talking about method rather than transformational trends.

In order to innovate, you need a method. But simply layering methods of innovation on old structures is counterproductive.

Innovation, as a movement, has become a search for methods for improving the existing model of business.

Innovation choices, such as ideation platforms or Six Sigma, or even open innovation all have substantial value but they are not a route to the breakthrough required to be a winner in the 21st century.

They work well within the existing wealth creation models but ironically innovation efforts often become a vehicle for reinforcing the status quo.

The innovation that companies need is fundamental, systemic and transformational.

Their dilemma is not about a search for new ideas. Most companies have access to plenty of ideas. It is about adapting to radically new business conditions and opportunities. Right now, business needs to make a leap to the elastic enterprise.

The elastic enterprises that we discuss in this book are transformational. They produce breakthrough business processes, concepts, products and services.

When elastic enterprises innovate they do not do it piecemeal or incrementally, nor do they innovate simply to beat the competition. They innovate to alter or control market conditions in new ways.

Every company and every organization has access to the capabilities that elastic enterprises have pioneered.

The common thread running through all business and organizational life is the ability to exploit a convergence of network technology, mobility and human ecosystems, supported by business platforms and universal connectors. Together these dynamics help to renew the system of wealth creation and to rebuild competitiveness on a completely different scale, at an entirely new pace.

Built into the system are techniques that allow large numbers of contractual business relationships to develop at little overhead cost, either in terms of the legal process of establishing business relationships or the emotional cost of managing them. Those 300,000 developer contracts Apple has—they were created automatically, at least in the legalistic sense. Driving business friction out is an important new, competitive weapon.

These platforms and ecosystems are quickly being augmented by Cloud computing.

For example, USAA, the giant U.S. insurer, was able to put together a profitable and extremely compelling new service that provides customers with comparative data on actual car purchase prices. Imagine being able to buy a car knowing what other people are actually paying. It worked for USAA, so within a year of its car data service opening for business, it moved on and created a second adjacent service providing comparative data on actual house purchase prices.

Put together at low cost, these ecosystem businesses can also be broken down quickly. It provides a level of agility few would have dreamed of until recently.

The Elastic Enterprise documents and interprets these developments and suggests ways that executives can build on them[5]. While *The Elastic Enterprise* is a result of our research observations and thinking, it's not the final word, it's just the beginning. Even at this stage though it is apparent that key identifiable differences in operating models separate winners from losers.

THE MAINPOINTS REVIEWED:

Highly competitive companies have prospered through the tough years by transforming their basic operational processes, by becoming *elastic*.

The elastic enterprise can scale its operations without a parallel increase in overhead. These are the new scale economics—growth without a crippling increase in complexity management.

In the new global market companies must also serve customer markets in new ways, they must address mass differentiation, they must segment markets in new ways and create the capacity to serve many micro-markets, globally.

Successful companies have gone beyond innovation to transformation. To remain competitive every company needs to adopt a simple transformational model that we will explain in the coming chapters.

To get a feel for how close you are to an elastic enterprise or how big a cultural shift awaits it is useful to ask:

1. Is our operating model adaptable or fixed?
2. How do we initiate process transformation? Outside in, or, inside out?

3. Do we focus our innovation efforts mostly on methods for how to improve our products and services?

4. Who do we use as models for how to grow our business?

5. Do we benchmark or do we seek transformational opportunities?

6. Are we in the key performance indicators game or do we have a more conceptual approach to assessing our future prospects?

7. What type of thought leadership do we aspire to?

8. How closely aligned is our IT department with our business objectives?

9. Is there conflict between IT and business or are we using the CIO office strategically to promote growth?

10. How well do we understand global markets?

11. Do we have access to micro-markets?

12. What hyper channel strategies do we have?

13. Do we think about APIs and their role in hyper channel strategies?

---

[1] Consider also that during the period 2000 to 2010, the number of users on the Internet grew by approximately 445% with Africa leading the way at 2,357%, followed by the Middle East at 1,825% and Latin America at 1,033%. All other regions of the world grew at levels well under 1,000%. When considered in absolute terms, the number of users on the Internet are led by Asia at 825.1 million, Europe at 475.1 million, followed by North America at 266.2 million with the remaining approximately 600 million distributed across other geographies.

[2] Eric D. Beinhocker, Diana Farrell and Adil S. Zainulbhai, "Tracking The Growth of India's Middle Class," *McKinsey Quarterly*, August 2007.

[3] For example, Hans Rosling (see http://www.youtube.com/watch?v=jbkSRLYSojo), a noted authority on global health and development and statistician, also sees continued global economic growth. However, he like others, such as Dani Rodrik (see http://rodrik.typepad.com/dani_rodriks_weblog/2007/11/doing-growth-di.html), also see a variety of impediments that must be solved for long-term sustainability, such as health, education, marketable skill development, new forms of energy, and sustainable population growth, and,

most important, long-term level of investment. See also the UN's Millennium Development Goals (www.un.org/millenniumgoals/reports.shtml).

[4] The advantages of the economics of scale and its relationship to productivity and growth are well understood, having formed the foundations of the industrial business model. However, an opposing and vexing issue, often not discussed, is the problem of diseconomies of scale. Diseconomies of scale refer to the inability of scale enterprises (i.e., large organizations) to nurture and support small-scale activities.

[5] Haydn Shaughnessy and Nick Vitalari, *Succeeding in the Age of HyperInnovation,* Moxie Insight, 2011; Nicholas Vitalari, *Platform Business: Outpacing Competitors and Harnessing the Global Community,* Moxie Insight, 2011; Nicholas Vitalari and Laura Carrillo, *IT Management in a Next Generation Enterprise,* nGenera, 2009; Haydn Shaughnessy, *Rethinking the Brand in the Age of Consumer Empowerment,* nGenera, 2009; Haydn Shaughnessy, *Open Management and the Enterprise Ecosystem,* nGenera, 2010; Jeff DeChambeau, Naumi Haque, Nicholas Vitalari, *Continuous Strategy for a Networked World,* Moxie Insight, 2010.

CHAPTER 2
THE RADICAL ROAD TO GROWTH

Elasticity is a potential source of competitive advantage. But to realize it, leaders need to know what is changing in their economic environment.

During the last 100 years, experience and conventional wisdom suggested that an increase in the scale of the enterprise led to less flexibility and cumbersome rigidity in strategy, execution, and change. In most cases that has proved true.

Scale has also proved to be corrosive to organic growth. As the scale of revenue grows the amount of additional revenue required to achieve a material impact on the enterprise's growth rate often discourages organic growth options. Organic methods of growth are abandoned in favor of mergers or acquisitions with scale revenue streams that will noticeably impact the revenue growth.

Increasing scale has also been associated with complexity and coordination costs. Many of the labor inputs for a large global corporation are spent on administrative and managerial activity to manage and coordinate resources.

For example, in the case of the management of IT, as the portfolio of information systems grows, more effort and cost is spent on maintaining systems rather than adding or creating new systems that support new business initiatives or ventures. The same is true in other functional areas.

But as we moved further into the 21st century, a number of companies emerged that seemed to contradict the prevailing experience regarding scale and elasticity.

From Book Seller to Elastic Enterprise

Amazon.com began life back in 1995 as an online bookstore and, according to some accounts, a "regret minimization framework" for founder Jeff Bezos, who was worried about missing the Internet gold rush.

Amazon quickly developed into a formidable competitor in the book trade, taking on entrenched category players like Barnes & Noble, and Borders, ultimately decimating their businesses and transforming the publishing industry.

But the real story of Amazon is its elasticity.

From its founding in 1995 to its current multi-product, multi-industry business model and acquisition strategy, Amazon has demonstrated a remarkable ability to drive rapidly into new business segments, offer new and innovative services, and introduce products and services of its own making.

Almost every move into a new market segment, a new product area or an entirely new line of business has added to profits and increased Amazon's competitiveness.

In two cases, Amazon's adjacencies transformed key industries and introduced novel business models.

The introduction of the Kindle, whose story is still not finished, radically changed buying habits, reading behavior and distribution of published works, as well as the fundamental economics of the publishing industry. Amazon is following up its early Kindle success by becoming a publisher itself through Kindle Direct.

In a totally unrelated arena, Amazon's continuous innovation in electronic commerce eventually lead to "cloud services," making it a vanguard company shaping one of the fastest-growing segments in the IT services industry.

During all of this growth and innovation, Amazon has not missed a beat in terms of execution, customer service and expansion of its business.

These moves are examples of what we call radical adjacency. They are not just minor adjacencies that we've seen throw even well run organizations off-balance. These are major market-creating or market-disrupting moves. And they are executed with aplomb. Radical adjacency is new. And it is among the most disruptive activities in today's markets.

Would you bet against Amazon? Is there a limit to its ambition or its ability to move at will into new markets, new industries, and new product lines? Amazon appears to be very comfortable and positioned to exploit the continued expansion of a global, digitally enhanced marketplace. While it may suffer lower margins in the short-term, in the service of organic growth, its business models, infrastructure and leadership seem well tuned for contemporary business realities. Amazon is an elastic enterprise able to scale new enterprise opportunities almost at will.

Amazon.com began its spectacular ascent through the ranks of modern businesses when its customers became reviewers, first of books and then of other products. Remember that whole meme around customers as recommenders?

But where Amazon really began to take off as a 21st-century enterprise was when customers—not just Amazon's but that whole cohort of consumers who were reaching for a more creative lifestyle—became *writers*. Amazon's current phase of growth is built on the customer community as creative artists.

Consider this: Did the Kindle come first or did the writers come first? Did one device create the self-publishing industry or was there huge pent-up creativity looking for an outlet?

One of the first self-published authors, Amanda Hocking, wrote about vampires and sold over 100,000 copies per month.

Hocking illustrates many hidden truths of the new business climate. Customers are creative. Creative people are closer to a wider range of strong market niches than companies ever can be. Those creative people can form an invaluable business ecosystem. Platforms that support the exploitation of widely diffused creative talent can be hugely successful.

Platforms and Ecosystems—The Rise of Scaled Interaction

There is a rule in the natural world that says that as natural systems scale, the energy that nature expends on sustaining them decreases proportionally. In other words, as a forest or wetland or a human or animal grows it becomes cheaper and easier to sustain, in terms of the natural inputs of light, water, protein, nitrogen and so on.

Scale in natural systems is efficient.

The big difference between natural systems and human-social systems is that when human-social systems scale they inevitably absorb proportionally more energy. To grow human-social systems, like growing an enterprise, is costly. But it is not only costly. Ultimately the cost of building a human-social system will reach a point where the cost of scale outweighs the benefits.

Humans naturally find ways to handle scale, particularly when they overreach and find their limits. They reduce costs. Streamline operations. Lease assets rather than buy them. Divest. Reengineer. Retreat. Or simply scale back. Humans have done so repeatedly throughout history.[1]

It's not so crystal clear, however, that cost cutting or re-scaling today is contributing to a vibrant business community—employees, customers, shareholders, partners and suppliers. Something in the mix is wrong and not producing the desired results.

The factory system of production and the bureaucratic office system of service provision both provided economies of scale, scale fit for purpose in their day.

For over 200 years they provided wealth-enhancing growth, driven by generations of product innovation.

But at a certain point the advantages of scale began to diminish, due to a rise in the administrative overhead, transaction costs incurred in managing humans at scale, and lately a lack of core scientific invention to alleviate those increased costs.

Nonetheless, many companies still function with these classic human "operating systems."

Everything we are taught about economics means we cling to them rather than go through the pain of cognitive reframing, the re-imagining of how we should go about creating wealth.

We have assumed from the days of Adam Smith that the division of labor into small, discreet work tasks gives us a wealth-creation system based on economies that can scale into large factories. And we have exploited specialization for over 200 years, but with progressively less success in managing the overhead cost of scale.

Over the past 20 years the overhead of doing business at scale has begun to present new challenges as companies seek to lower their cost base continuously while pursuing opportunities in global markets.

In effect we have been relying on a 200 year old theory of rational economic behavior to guide us, even though Smith was writing at a time when much of what passed for industry was community-based and highly localized.

Ginzberg and Vojta wrote *Beyond Human Scale*[2], an indictment of centralized management, over 25 years ago. Companies have tried to address that challenge but the forces of globalization mean we now have bigger organizations that perceive a need for stronger centralized controls.

By 2010, the household products group at Procter & Gamble required extra revenue of approximately $8 billion a year to sustain double-digit growth. At the low end of start-up funding, that represents about 400,000 new businesses per year.

Gregory Milano's company, Fortuna Advisors, studied the comparative returns and growth performance of large, medium and smaller companies in the top 1000 U.S. corporations.

There was hardly a measure that showed size, as conventionally understood, to be an advantage. Total shareholder returns of large firms were nearly 70% below that of the smaller firms over a 10-year period. Share price performance was 25% lower. Larger firms were also more likely to redistribute cash back to shareholders, which itself exposes the firm to more future performance risk.[3]

Look around your enterprise and ask yourself if this is the case.

Has your organization reached that tipping point between efficient growth and sclerotic scale? Many global organizations are there, beyond the tipping point. They've been there for quite a while, despite laudable attempts to change, to become lean, or to decouple and decentralize.

Perhaps your company does not fit into this category, but many do.

Many companies persist in the belief that traditional or "brute force" industrial-style scale brings valuable economies. In the modern world we see those strategies succeeding but at a high human cost, exemplified by the human resource problems of companies like Foxconn in China. Yes, brute force management can work but it is morally questionable. The brute force argument though is expressed in numerous ways.

CFO Magazine quotes AT&T CEO Rick Lindner at the time of AT&T's now failed acquisition of T-Mobile from Deutsche Telekom as saying; "The scale and the combination of operational assets provide us with a path to industry-leading wireless margins. The synergies available from this combination are substantial, with a net present value that exceeds the purchase price."[4]

This is illusory talk. The reality of AT&T and T-Mobile's business was extreme pressure on margins, driving competitor companies like Ericsson and Nokia Siemens Networks to reinvent themselves or risk being consumed by Chinese competition. To assume industry-leading margins in the most competitive of industries was an old-school moment and a mistake.[5]

The elastic enterprise offers a new solution, based around business platforms and business ecosystems.

We call it *the economies of scaled interaction,* or simply, *elastic scale.* And elastic scale is what we need; it is the appropriate form of human organization for today.

Whereas previous economies of scale rested on factory operating systems, or office bureaucracies, the elastic enterprise rest on five unique dynamics, which we will define briefly now:

1. **The business platform:** a collection of transparent rules, software and relationships for ingesting contributions to a business opportunity (apps, content, services) and for channeling those to a customer base,
2. **The business ecosystem:** the collection of interacting participants in the platform (developers, customers, partners, owner), including third party actors like information providers,
3. **Universal connectors:** technologies and rules that allow the friction-free formation of business relationships (e.g. RSS, APIs),
4. **The Cloud:** infrastructure (elastic access to storage, computing power and services as needed), and
5. **Sapient leadership**: new leadership behaviors that are highly responsive to and respected by peers outside the company.

These five dynamics make the interaction among humans and organizations more fluid and creative, more productive and more adaptable, than could ever be achieved in a factory or an office. The most developed of these dynamics today are the business platform and the business ecosystem, along with the system of universal connectors that allow scaled interaction to take place at low cost.

The business platform is a key term and a key capability in the elastic enterprise.

We tend to think of the business platform as a concept loaded with bad connotations. Over the past 25 years it has been associated with customer lock-in, especially in big ERP systems or airline reservation systems, for example. But the new breed of business platform presents huge benefits in an elastic business environment and is not at all associated with lock-in.

This new platform's essence lies in its ability to scale interaction between companies, institutions, humans and machines. The business platform works with the business ecosystem, the second of the five dynamics, to enable the elastic enterprise to orchestrate a range of friction-free bilateral relationships.

Think of Apple and its apps developers. Think of Amazon and its commerce engine driven by reviewers and now writers. Think of Salesforce.com and its Force network of partners. Think of Facebook and its 800+ million members and countless companies using the Facebook business platform and business ecosystem.

Or think of Zynga using multiple social network platforms for gaming. Or Bunchball's business platform that supports the gamification of enterprises. Or, SCVNGR that builds on the Google Maps platform and the Google Places API to gamify everyday life for individuals and enterprises. What about Google and the millions of people who use its search engine as an advertising platform?

The common thread of these examples is they involve many thousands of business contracts, all of them conducted anonymously, with no meetings at the club, no handshake, no knowledge of where you went to school or who your parents know. This is anonymous, friction-free business, scalable in an instant and at an ultra-low cost compared to old ways of doing business.

Are we simply talking about the power effects of network technologies?

After all, we know that networks conform to power laws, which is to say they exhibit extraordinary growth potential. A typical power law case might be a YouTube video that ramps up from a few hundred viewers to a several million in a short span of time. Liked entities or objects, online, attract more likes and produce this power effect.

But the outcomes of the power law are random—in the sense that you never really know which product, or content, is going to go into orbit.

What we are talking about with the elastic enterprise is a predictable, structured approach to business, one that will never escape random effects but which is in fact a new operating system for human wealth creation, as palpable as the factory or bureaucracy.

More Than a Network Effect

We have to dig deeper than the network effect to understand the power of friction-free bilateral relationships and the power of the elastic enterprise.

In traditional business models, the enterprise is structured to produce for a given capacity. Efficiency comes from wringing increasing levels of output from that capacity. Extra capacity is added when the existing output reaches a computed maximum relative to demand.

That also means that most investment decisions are made on a marginal basis, at the tipping point where anticipated demand looks likely to push production capacity into a new phase of enterprise scale.

The old example of this is a factory that reaches capacity. The factory owner anticipates 10% additional demand in the following year. But at this extra margin of demand, it is necessary to build a new factory. The cost is going to be well in excess of what a 10% increase in demand justifies.

This type of scale doesn't disappear in the elastic era but it is mitigated by wide ranging supply agreements for the production of physical product and sophisticated management of global sourcing.[6] And in soft products (content, software, apps, software services) it does disappear. Here scale is set free from physical investment constraints.

The elastic enterprise takes advantage of the business ecosystem and platform, tools and organizing structures that are capable of exploiting the business value chain more effectively.

An example will help to clarify their role.

Google's AdWords is a first rate platform and ecosystem model.

The AdWords/AdSense business ecosystem has created significant knowledge and skills around the capacity of website content to earn revenues for Google and the millions of companies who use Google's core products.

Look at the free-flowing ecosystem of search engine optimization, and organic content experts that effectively market Google's Ad Words and AdSense products (its highly effective text advertising services that you see on most web sites) on Google's behalf.

Google manages this huge knowledge ecosystem with the lightest possible touch, doing a spectacular job of turning SEO and SEM (Search Engine Optimization, Search Engine Marketing) into a game where experts try to second-guess the Google algorithm each and every day. An SEO/SEM expert conveys to a global audience that they have the secret that can get client products to the top of Google rankings, or place effective text ads alongside search results.

In doing so they sell Google to customers across the globe.

This is an example of a business ecosystem (search engine optimizers and their clients) and a platform (AdWords, the text ad distribution platform that delivers contextual ads to websites in real time, at extraordinary scale).

The existence of dynamic *business ecosystems* like this, where huge communities of businesses act in concert, is part of the reason why the elastic enterprise comes closest to the natural laws of scaling we noted earlier.

The elastic enterprise employs tools, systems and ideas that make scale cheaper and more elastic than it would be otherwise.

Scale and Radical Adjacency

When we began researching elastic enterprises, one of the phenomena we noticed early on was a tendency of elastic enterprises to move quickly into adjacent markets.

It seems that the new ability to organize interactions at scale, based around the five dynamics we mentioned above, allows companies to accomplish what is generally regarded as one of the most difficult business strategies of all—to move into markets where an executive team has limited knowledge, experience and skills.

But look at Apple. It has been able to extend into many new markets. It has grown through its new elasticity. And that elasticity has allowed it to develop a new adjacent business strategy that has taken it into music, video, advertising, publishing, autos and the home. The Guardian newspaper is extending into product areas like search. Forbes is moving into book publishing.

Naturally these companies have to hire executives with expertise in those areas to make a success of radical adjacency or quickly forge new partnerships. But every company plotting adjacency moves can hire.

Most adjacencies fail on the grounds of cultural misalignment. The company's culture is simply unable to cope with a new market or geography.

The difference in Apple's case is that its culture has been reframed by its leaders to make radical adjacency seem natural. And its core competency has shifted out of computing into the development and management of highly scaled interaction.

Amazon too has been a poster child for radical adjacency. Apple and Amazon have used the new form of scale to enter new markets very successfully, over and over.

Traditional companies ordinarily find one adjacency very challenging. And industrial conglomerates that operate in multiple industries often focus on one core competency or at most 2–3 core competencies.

In fact, business case studies are full of attempts to create successful adjacencies. UK cement maker, Blue Circle Cement's ill-fated move into lawnmowers to diversify and grow, Cisco's defunct move into video cameras (Flip), Sears and Roebuck's dilutive attempt at retail finance and real estate with acquisitions of Dean Witter and Caldwell Banker, and Kodak's unlikely purchase of Sterling Drug.

A five-year study of adjacencies by Bain & Company of 1,850 companies showed that only 13% achieved what Bain called "even a modest level of sustained and profitable growth.⁷"

We are now 20 years into the Internet revolution. Such revolutions usually play out through a series of transformations that eventually culminate in a classic s-shaped curve over a 50-year period. In other words, we should be seeing the first corporations exhibiting peak performance through their use of the Internet. And in a limited number of cases that is what we are beginning to see.

Adopting elastic business structures would be futile without a good sense of transformational trends. Here too companies can be in denial. They might acknowledge that there is a "new normal" but they attribute that to the recession, not to fundamental changes in business conditions (which might actually have created or contributed to recession).

Our view is the new normal began 20 years ago. But most companies are still operating in the old normal.

Even if they have web or Internet strategies, they might not have woken up to the new phase of globalization—being led by frontier countries; or the impact of new consumer empowerment—new levels of market differentiation. The new normal is also radical adjacency and the implications of elastic enterprises entering new markets at will.

The reality is that elastic enterprises are responding to changing conditions. One way they are doing that is by creating new markets and invading and disrupting old markets, the essence of radical adjacency. Instead of buckling under the strains of minor adjacencies they are thriving through being radical.

THE MAIN POINTS REVIEWED:

Elastic enterprises have capabilities that set them apart from companies operating under an old industrial model. Principal among these is their ability to move seamlessly into adjacent markets.
We call this radical adjacency to indicate its dramatic effect.

Business platforms enable elastic enterprises to make radical adjacency moves. These two elements together, the platform and radical adjacency become the new core competency.

They allow companies to move to a new scale economics, moving beyond scale based around specialization to scale based on human interaction management.

To get a feel for how acquainted you already are with these issues ask:

1. How dependent are we on closed platforms, or single vendor proprietary information systems, like ERP systems?

2. Do we have a gamification strategy?

3. How ambitious are we with our growth plans?

4. Is our social media exposure teaching us how to interact with the external environment more competently?

5. Are we comfortable co-creating with very large number of partners?

6. Are we engaged only with the people we know best, like our employees or a small group of trusted suppliers?

7. Do we still rely on agencies to communicate with the world?

8. When was the last time we attempted an adjacency move?

9. Did my company get taken by surprise by the "Bring Your Own Device" movement?

10. What is our customer ecosystem? Do we have one?

11. When was the last time we altered a key process?

12. Are we willing to critically evaluate our business models?
13. How do we go about realigning our governance models, decision rights and authority structures?
14. How do we manage stakeholder relationships?
15. How do we cultivate and manage weak ties?
16. Do we aspire to meet analyst expectations or radically exceed all expectations?

---

[1] The conundrum of scale in human collectives has been at the root of commercial and political revolutions. The effectiveness of the Roman Empire rested on new innovations in the organization of human talent that was superior at scale relative to other civilizations at the time. The more recent debates between markets, capitalist and Marxist-derived human collectives, all revolve around the means of production, and the allocation of resources to the means of production. It has long been known that scale economics determine the success of economies and the wealth of nations.

[2] Eli Ginzberg and George Vojta, *Beyond Human Scale: The Large Corporation at Risk*. New York: Basic Books, 1986.

[3] Gregory V. Milano, "Too Big to Succeed?" *CFO Magazine*, April 29, 2011.

[4] Ibid.

[5] ibid.

[6] For example, Apple is known co-develop and to buy the entire production capacity of a supplier or fund the initial ramp up and production of a new non-proprietary component, particularly with companies that source an innovative or breakthrough component that Apple wants in its product. In this way Apple precludes competitors from acquiring that component. Apple will also corner production on what it feels will be high demand components or tooling to protect its supply chain and production schedules. It will also alternate suppliers as it did by going with Pegatron for its CDMA iPhone 4 versus Foxconn, its primary supplier for the prior iPhone releases in Shenzhen, China. For further reading see "Apple Supply Chain Secrets Revealed," Times of India, http://articles.timesofindia.indiatimes.com/2011-11-04/infrastructure/30358919_1_apple-software-tim-cook-jony-ive

[7] Chris Zook, *Beyond the Core: Expand Your Market Without Abandoning Your Roots*. Boston: Harvard Business School Press, 2004.

CHAPTER 3
CREATING THE ELASTIC ENTERPRISE

The Road to Transformation

When Larry Page and Sergey Brin left Stanford University and started Google in 1998, their goal was to index the Internet so it could be effectively searched by anyone.

A more relevant search engine for digital artifacts, whether text, graphics, pictures or video, had escaped the best minds in computer science for decades. Google's rating-based computational approach revolutionized the search industry. What did it do? It used the global ecosystem of search engine users to continuously update and refine an evaluation system. By scoring relevance according to how people linked pages on the web, the behavior of millions of anonymous content providers and users created the system of page rankings. That in turn made search results more relevant to search users.

After establishing Page Rank, Google introduced AdWords, the adverts that you see alongside search results and alongside web content.

AdWords encouraged a generation of content producers everywhere to believe they could build sustainable revenues from putting their content on the web.

It fuelled the dramatic growth of blogging and web site development.

From a standing start in 2003, hobbyists and experts all over the world launched themselves onto the web with a Wordpress blog and an AdWords sidebar. By mid-decade, bloggers were pushing 1 million posts per day onto the web in the English language alone.

Google was a central feature in blogging's boom because it tied production of content to advertising, giving advertisers access to truly niche markets and encouraging content producers to seek revenue.

The intent and aspirations of Brin and Page at the outset though were not to revolutionize the computer and information science sector, nor to completely transform advertising, nor to destabilize the news industry, nor to create a Google-plex that would enable it to integrate a myriad of unrelated industries at will and to monetize seemingly unrelated acquisitions like Blogger and Google Maps.

Douglas Edwards notes in his insider account of Google,[1] "You would have needed uncanny foresight or powerful pharmaceuticals to envision Google's success in 1999."

And by the way, remember that Jeff Bezos, the visionary founder of Amazon, also did not intend to revolutionize the publishing industry, introduce the Kindle or restructure the IT services sector with its EC2 (Elastic Compute Cloud) or AWS (Amazon Web Services).

He had a more modest proposition: use the Internet to revolutionize the consumer retail business.

While broad and ambitious, it in no way accounts for the diversified global business that characterizes Amazon today.

But, regardless of intents and aspirations, all three companies (Google, Apple and Amazon), along with many others like eBay, Alibaba, PayPal, Skype, and lately old industry stalwarts like USAA, MasterCard, Caterpillar, Ford and GM, created new structures for how they interact with markets.

Each has adopted one or more of the five dynamics of the elastic enterprise.

The elastic enterprise rests on five distinct interlocking capabilities. We call them *dynamics* because the elastic enterprise is not bounded as enterprises have been historically.

Rather, elastic enterprises are permeable and in motion.

They intersect and interact with their partners and customers.

The exhibit a type of fluidity founded on the power of relationships, amplified by a network of instantaneous connections.

In combination, the five dynamics produce unprecedented strategic, operational and competitive capabilities.

FIGURE 3.1 The Five Dynamics of the Elastic Enterprise

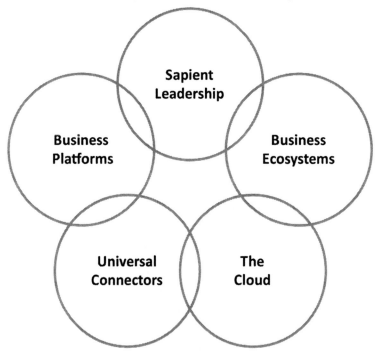

Early experience indicates that the process of combining these five dynamics dramatically assists enterprises to develop next-generation business models. As the subtitle of *The Elastic Enterprise* suggests, we think of this as a revolution in business. But it is not just about re-engineering business processes. It is about re-conceiving how we scale and operate businesses in the 21st Century.

We want to illustrate now how the five dynamics transport the enterprise to a whole new level of scale, efficiency and effectiveness. Coming up in subsequent chapters—more detail on the dynamics and case studies to illustrate their impact.

The Digital Transformation of Business

For over a decade IT and business functions have been at odds in many organizations. Many people in a typical organization might even think of IT as a drag on change. IT policy, IT systems, and IT rules, seem to confine and constrain dynamic activity. But that era is over, the elastic enterprise brings IT and business functions back together. The elastic enterprise drives a culturally anchored transformation of IT and its role.

The technological underpinnings of a business radically change when companies adopt elastic principles. So much so that elastic enterprises use different software architectures in their operations and are transforming the Business-IT relationship in the process.

IT has always held out the promise of transformation and as we said earlier the combination of internal IT systems modeled on web-like structures is beginning to fulfill that promise. Here's a little background.

The first use of computerized information technology in business was at the General Electric Appliance plant in 1954. Information technology progressed rapidly through the 1950s and 60s, dominated by large mainframe computers with systems focused on financial, accounting applications and reporting-based systems for manufacturing and sales.

The 1970s and 80s saw the emergence of minicomputers and personal computers, respectively. In the process most large companies developed large portfolios of customized software applications and complex computing infrastructures operated by professional IT units. This triggered the process of IT-Business separation.

In the 1990s packaged software, as an alternative to custom developed software emerged.

But the 90s also saw the arrival of the Internet and eCommerce. By the end of the 1990s a new paradigm was emerging.

Thought leaders, like Don Tapscott, began to highlight the impact of global webs of businesses, operating in a seemingly collaborative way.[2]

Three distinct developments, though, altered the computational landscape for corporations.

These three pivotal developments are still relatively new. Their implications are still in the works. We know they are hugely powerful but their ultimate impact will not be known for decades. These developments are powering the new phase of globalization and business transformation.

First, the emergence of mobile devices and related telecommunications infrastructure extends individual access to computing and Internet-related services to virtually every location on the planet. Today's start-up hotspots for example are Nairobi and Istanbul, and Silicon Valley investors are working there with local entrepreneurs who are now connected via mobile and wireless into the global entrepreneur community.

Second, the proliferating interconnections among computers and computing infrastructure led to the emergence of Cloud computing. Cloud computing has become a catch-all term for making computational power, capacity and related services available to anyone, anywhere at any time.

Third, software has changed radically. New programming languages, new standards for data interchange and new standards for the way information is presented to the user have led to a new flexibility in the assembly of systems.

These three developments set the stage for a completely different type of computing infrastructure and a new computing services infrastructure.

Many companies find it difficult to make a transition to this new computational era. But to understand why the elastic enterprise is possible requires a deeper examination of it.

For most of the last 50 years, corporations were forced to make private investments in large-scale information technology projects to meet their business objectives. Often these IT projects required significant customization or new code written from scratch, in-house. For example, Walmart spent over $300 million in 1990 to create its much-vaunted logistics system, most of which was written by employees at its HQ in Bentonville, Arkansas.

Even where existing commercial software packages might meet business objectives, most companies were forced to engage in an arduous and often dubious effort to customize "out-of-the-box" packaged software to meet their unique needs, and then continue to modify the code over its useful life as business requirements evolved. These practices also meant that IT had to support internal users through expensive to maintain internal help desks, that implemented rules and policies that employees typically resented.

As the 21st century debuted, following billions of dollars that organizations of all sizes were forced to spend on the "Millennium Bug," many IT departments were viewed as a "business prevention department" rather than a strategic resource. Commentators like Nicholas Carr argued[3] that IT didn't matter any more because information technology had become a commodity and would soon become a generalized utility lending little to no competitive advantage to most firms.

Over this same period, an alternative approach to information technology began to emerge. This one was inspired by an old notion of interchangeable parts and modular assemblies. This was sometimes called *object-oriented,* which simply means the focal point is a re-usable component of software that can be connected to other reusable components, rather than a large enterprise package.

While object-oriented computing can trace its roots to academia and other research laboratories, the growth of this "interchangeable parts" approach to software was very much driven by the Internet and its needs, and it grew in significance as the web replaced the Internet as the main platform of online activity.

It began with a change in programming languages, starting with object-oriented languages and then moving to easy to use "scripting languages" that at a rather "atomic level" introduced a new level of flexibility.

With languages like JavaScript, PHP, and Ruby on Rails for example, program components can be bound together at the time of use (i.e. execution) rather than in advance, providing radical new architectural flexibility for system designers. In simple terms, because the operation of the program is determined at the time of use, various components can be assembled based on each unique user's requirement when needed.

Also, standards like XML (a standard for data interchange) and HTML (a standard for presentation used in web browsers) enabled developers to feed data to different systems and programs and allowed different devices (e.g. PCs, Macs, tablets, phones) to present the same information in similar formats.

These standards were not formed in a vacuum or without considerable effort from industry experts, governments and cross-company collaboration. Nor have such efforts ended.

The Internet enabled basic interconnectivity, but a more substantial layer of standards was required for true, so-called, "industrial strength" cross-vendor, cross-machine and cross-network interoperability.

While it is not our purpose to dive into technical detail, we do want to call out some important international efforts.

For example, W3C (the World Wide Web Consortium) initiated by Tim Berners-Lee has worked to make the web open and available to everyone so that all devices can interoperate "by developing protocols and guidelines that ensure the long-term growth of the Web."[4]

Other international consortiums like OASIS (Organization for the Advancement of Structured Information Standards) create many standards for data interchange, exchange of GPS information, emergency information, building information, messaging, alerts and a plethora of other types of standards essential for open computing use.[5]

And more recently, an outgrowth of work from OASIS has led to a specific working group TOSCA (Topology and Orchestration Specification for Cloud Applications) focused on international standards for the Cloud[6] that will ultimately enable companies and institutions to offer business services using a standardized format and structure.

TOSCA and subsequent work will enable a true global services marketplace to emerge that will someday permit the assembly of virtually limitless combinations of business offerings, on demand.

Today, we are just beginning to operate in this new flexible computing environment. And as more investment goes into the Cloud, that in turn further extends the power of the Internet and the web, the flexibility will only increase.[7]

Even at this stage, there are virtually no barriers to any business or individual participating on the web if they have software development capabilities and the appropriate technical knowledge to match their aspirations.

As a consequence we have a rapidly developing global community participating in global platforms and creating content or objects on remote servers in collaboration with many thousands of people. The web, with its new apps, social networks, mobile apps and devices, and a growing digital literacy establish a compelling and fundamentally new computing landscape.

FIGURE 3.2 Contributors to the New Computing Landscape

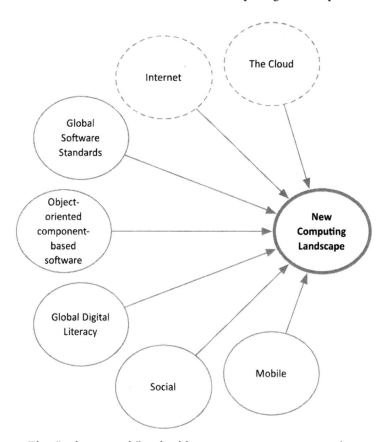

This "web approach" to building systems, using an interchangeable or modular architecture, has transformed the way business systems are designed.

Systems capabilities for businesses can now be assembled from a variety of components. The need for custom code has been reduced significantly—and a major source of entry cost, rework and ongoing cost of ownership has ben be reduced.

In its own way it is a revolution in information technology. Most importantly, it has given rise to the new business platform.

The business platform is one of the most powerful dynamics in the elastic enterprise.

Dynamic One: Business Platforms

A business platform is a package of accessible interconnected digital components (hardware and software) that together deliver a set of business services[8].

The primary objective of those services is the scaled interaction we talked about in Chapter 1, between people anywhere, along with the information they need to be effective, and the commerce engine that accrues revenue to the platform owner and its partners.

Think about that long legacy of software that Nicholas Carr talked about in *Does IT Matter*, and the massive investments in IT infrastructure by each and every firm.

Each enterprise used to have (and still has) its own portfolio of information systems and hardware, and had to manage and modify it to meet its unique and changing needs.

But as we discussed in the previous section, we now have the ability to instantaneously connect people, machines, software components and entire organizations at will.

And we have the ability to develop and assemble business platforms, like iTunes, Facebook, Google Maps, YouTube, Google+, Salesforce. com, LinkedIn, Netflix, or USAA's AutoCircle. This is the "new IT."

In fact IT and the business become fused together again through business platforms, driving a singularity and clarity of purpose in the enterprise.

The ability to fuse a company's diverse talents, technical and otherwise, around a profound purpose, through business platforms, is reflected in Apple's CEO Tim Cook comments about technical innovations like iCloud and Siri:

I would view iCloud not as something with a year or two product life; it's a strategy for the next decade or more. I think it's truly profound.

On Siri. You know, for years, if you were a PC or Mac user, you used a physical keyboard, and you used a mouse for input. And you pretty much did that for a long, long time. And there wasn't a great deal of—there was evolution in that space, but not a lot of revolution, really …

I think these two are both profound; they're not things where we run separate P&Ls on, because we don't do that—we don't believe in that.

We manage the company at the top and just have one P&L and don't worry about the iCloud team making money and the Siri team making money. We want to have a great customer experience, and we think measuring all these things at that level would never achieve such a thing. But I do think that both of these go in the profound category; they're not these things that will not mean anything a year or two from now. They're things that you will look back at, that you'll talk to your grandkids about, that were profound changes.[9]

If you look at Apple, Google, and Amazon this fusion of business and IT functions becomes apparent. The distinction has vanished amid the common pursuit of great products, information everywhere, and global retail.

Here's why.

On a strategic level, business platforms facilitate interaction between people, many of whom have a strong business purpose of their own. They do so in a transparent and open manner. Platforms do not discriminate on the basis of background, geography, income, ethnicity, or education. In fact they do not discriminate full stop. If you want to do business with a business platform, you simply need ideas, talent, and your own small resources.

On a pragmatic level, since the business platform is essentially a collection of interchangeable digital components, it has the capacity to be augmented and extended by adding or substituting *new* components.

Assuming the company has done its homework, each time its business platform is extended, the company adds new business features or services that enhance the customer value proposition, bring extra support to developers, or enable an entirely new business. There is no need for a fundamental remake of the business. As the quote from Tim Cook shows, profound change can take place *ON* the platform.

But of course it does more, as we already alluded to. It is all about interactivity at scale, where the cost of scale is low relative to the returns.

It actively enables the development of elastic global business ecosystems composed of productive partners that can collaborate with and contribute to the elastic enterprise's mission, in pursuit of their own goals.

In short the business platform becomes a critical unifying mechanism for the strategy and operation of an elastic enterprise and its partners.

FIGURE 3.3 The Virtuous Cycle of Business Platforms and Business Ecosystems

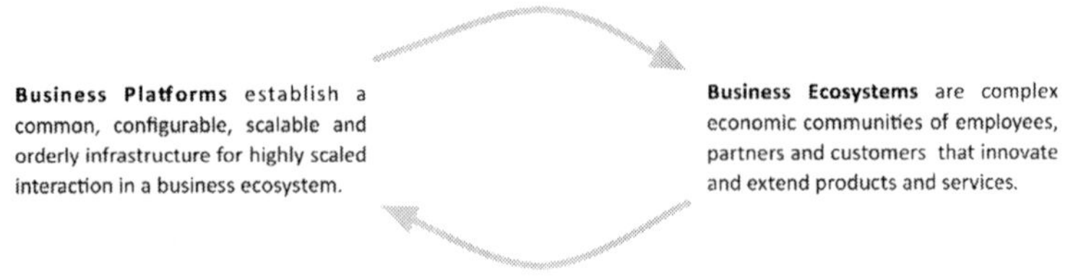

Business **Platforms** establish a common, configurable, scalable and orderly infrastructure for highly scaled interaction in a business ecosystem.

Business **Ecosystems** are complex economic communities of employees, partners and customers that innovate and extend products and services.

In an instantaneously connected world individuals and companies have a variety of relationships, some with strong ties and some with weak ties. In social networks like Facebook, or Google+, members have strong ties (e.g. family members, close friends, workmates) but they often have many more weak ties (e.g. acquaintances, people met at conferences, distant friends of friends).[10]

Business platforms enable companies to incorporate and transform weak-tie relationships into productive, value-added, revenue-producing business partnerships.

These largely anonymous business relationships work without a handshake or even an introduction. They function without social and traditional frictions because the business platform owner provides the structure and services for individuals and companies to engage with them, in a uniform way.

Different types of business platforms promote customer ecosystems, help manage large developer communities, incorporate supply chain partners, support e-commerce transactions, and engage employees in enterprise social networks.

And the trend is for business platforms to coordinate and transact with other external platforms like telemetry/sensor and telematics/telecommunication services, or specialized platforms for organizing platform-to-platform, machine-to-machine, or mobile-to-mobile activities, to name a few.

So, the business platform is like a global meeting place for ecosystems on both sides of the demand and supply chain. That might be its most ingenious character.

Whereas in the past proprietary closed platforms served a supply chain and a supplier community, today's business platforms pitch suppliers (developers) and customers together in an open community.

Apple's Elastic Business Platform in Action

Apple is the most successful implementation of a business platform. It holds lessons for any executive who wants to plot an elastic strategy.

Apple's business platform, as it currently exists, evolved over a period of more than a decade extending back into the 1990s before Steve Jobs re-entered Apple.

Beginning in the 1990s, like many other technology firms it cultivated a network of independent software developers to advise and create software for their core products. In Apple's case the developers coalesced around the Macintosh computer operating system (OS). It was a fairly small but loyal following.

On Steve Jobs return in 1997, the new CEO radically changed the direction of the Macintosh OS (operating system). This is important because it ultimately led Apple down a very fortuitous path and enabled a very flexible foundation for the evolution of the Macintosh, including the subsequent repurposing of the Mac OS in a different form as iOS, the operating system that underlies the iPhone, iTouch, iPad and Apple TV.

They replaced the old Macintosh OS with an industrial strength Mac OS based on a dialect of UNIX, originally developed at the University of California, Berkeley.

This "BSD Unix" was what Jobs used at his other start-up, NeXT.

They also employed Mach derivative components developed at Carnegie Melon University.[11]

On a parallel path, when it came to develop the iTunes server-based online business platform, Jobs repurposed other industrial strength capabilities. He did not build the now vast iTunes/App Store/iBooks business platform entirely on the Macintosh OS. Apple deployed the iTunes business platform on high performance server-grade technologies that could grow and expand over time.

While there are no specific public disclosures that we could find regarding the actual technical architecture of the platform, including iTunes and its supply chain network, one can surmise based on a review of public statements and hiring practices that it is probably based on a Unix variant, plus Apple's own WebObjects. It employs many industry standard components such as Dynamic HTML, HTML5, XML, MPEG, Ajax, Java, JavaScript, CSS to mention a few.

Since the iTunes Music Store was introduced, the company has been able to add new features, new capabilities, and new products to that business platform each year, with unprecedented speed and operational excellence.

Figures 3.3 and 3.4 chronicle the evolution of the Apple business platform from 2001–2006 when the iPod was introduced, and 2007–2012 after the iPhone and iPad were introduced.

A number of general lessons can be taken from this. First, companies looking to a platform strategy need to be very systematic in the way they plan, update and expand the architecture and related service capabilities.

Apple uses the iTunes business platform to introduce new business partners and their products into the Apple offer.

iTunes is also used as an integrative platform that coordinates the use of other business platforms such as the App Store, the iBook Store, and third party platforms like ATT's phone activation platform, and Nike's branded customer community.

One of more interesting early events in the evolution of the platform was the Nike+iPod venture formed between Apple and Nike in 2006.

Both firms learned a great deal about business platforms and customer ecosystems from this partnership.

For Nike+ they linked their respective business platforms to provide a new service to amateur runners. It allowed Nike to create a new value proposition for its customers by bringing them into a real-time customer ecosystem and branded community around its runner shoes and apparel. It became one of the largest branded online customer communities, in the world.

FIGURE **3.4** Evolution of the Apple Business Platform (2001–2006)

Year	Apple Business Platform Milestones
2000	SoundJam MP music player developed by Jeff Robbin and Bill Kincaid purchased by Apple and renamed iTunes. User interface changed and ability to burn CDs added
2001 (iPod Launched)	First Generation iPod Classic debuts, iTunes software package runs on Macintosh computers (bundled with Mac OS 9 first, then Mac OS X, version 10.0), 3Com's Kerbango Internet radio service bundled in iTunes, iTunes Versions 1.0 thru 2.0.3 released
2002	iPod Classic 2G, Audible.com audio books, 2nd Generation iPod, iTunes Versions 2.04 thru 4.0 released
2003 (Launch of iTunes Online Store, April 28)	iPod 3G, 200,000 from five major record labels, $.99/song sets industry standard, copy protection via FairPlay, Apple Digital Rights Management (DRM), AAC audio codec with encryption iTunes supports iPod, Macintosh OS and Microsoft Windows OS, ITunes Versions 4.0, thru 4.2
2004	iPod 4G, iPod Mini, More songs listed, conversion support for Microsoft WMA files to Apple AAC format, iMix, Apple Lossless, AirTunes, iTunes Versions 4.5, 4.6, 4.7 released
2005	iPod 5G, iPod Nano, iPod Shuffle, International iTunes stores debut, Video support, Podcasts, Video Podcasts, Photos, Sale of TV shows, iTunes Versions 4.7.1 thru 6.0.1 released
2006	Apple and Nike Alliance link iPod and Shoe motion sensor, Nike+iPod support introduced Transition to Intel processors for Macintosh computers, full length movies, games, iTunes Versions 6.0.2 thru 7.1.1 released

Mark McClusky discusses the history and lessons learned from the Nike+iPod in a 2009 Wired Magazine article:

> With such a huge group (of customers), Nike is learning things we've never known before. In the winter, people in the US run more often than those in Europe and Africa, but for shorter distances. The average duration of a run worldwide is 35 minutes, and the most popular Nike+ Powersong, which runners can set to give them extra motivation, is "Pump It" by the Black Eyed Peas.[12]

The venture thrives today for both companies. But Apple has moved on significantly.

Figures 3.4 and 3.5 show the public side of Apple's platform, but the company also uses private and largely undisclosed B2B business platforms that provide special services and product performance data, related to the design, testing and production of its products.

We also know that Apple's platform is integrated with its telecommunications carriers' partner business platforms and with inventory systems throughout the supply chain. It automates many of the business processes between these parties.

The platform also acts as a very powerful "intelligence network" and data acquisition engine for finding issues, diagnosing problems and identifying new use cases.

While external developers have always been a part of Apple's business the company's independent developer community mushroomed following the introduction of the iPhone in 2007. Figure 3.5 shows the evolution of the Apple business platform from 2007–2012. New features are added to iTunes, but significant new capabilities were added specifically to enhance the value proposition for developers, beginning in 2008.

The developers' platform includes iTunes, the iOS Software Development Kit (SDK), the Apple developer center (developer. apple.com) and the App Store.

Together these platforms provide the infrastructure and rules that let Apple work productively with a global community of independent businesses.

It means that, together, they can identify opportunities to generate revenue.

It also allows Apple to review developer products and compensate them for their contributions, again in a largely automated way.

After the iPad introduction in 2010, the capabilities of the platform expanded dramatically. Today iTunes manages sales contracts and customer contracts, music deals, subscriptions of many types, alerts and iCloud capabilities.

iTunes also enforces intellectual property rights and operates the marketplace for media and apps.

It provides an orderly marketplace for buyers and sellers of Apple products whether an independent software developer, a book writer, a magazine or newspaper publisher, a musician, a university, producer or a movie studio.

Apple has continued to integrate its business platform with each of its product lines and applications including iLife and iWork software collection and its Mail, iCal and Address Book applications. It also added a Mac App Store to the business platform in 2011. In February 2012, they announced the next version of the Macintosh OS, Mountain Lion, which will enable even more integration of services across all of the company's product lines.

When viewed holistically like this, you can begin to see the enormous power of the platform approach: The process automation, which significantly reduces business friction, the partner building (at low cost), the evolving competency in scaled interaction, and the capacity to innovate in every business context.

FIGURE 3.5 Evolution of the Apple Business Platform (2007–2012)

Year	Apple Business Platform Milestones
2007 (iPhone Launched)	iPhone, iTouch, iPod Classic 6G, iPod Nano 3G, Apple TV support added, iPhone online activation via iTunes, iTunes University launched, iTunes Music Store expanded, DRM-free music tracks added for $1.99, Ringtones added, iTunes Versions 7.1 thru 7.5 released
2008 (App Store Launched)	iPhone 3G, iTouch 2G, iPod Nano 4G, iPhone SDK, Apple Developer Center, App Store added, iPhone OS 2.0–2.01 support, iTunes movie rentals, Apple TV streaming, HD TV support, Genius automated playlists added, 10 Million apps downloaded in first 3 days, iTunes Versions 7.6 thru 8.0.2 released
2009	iPhone 3Gs, iTouch 3G, iPod Nano 5G, iPod Shuffle 3G, iPhone OS 3.0 support, Genius Mixes, Home Sharing, 1-click purchase, iTunes LPs, iTunes Extras, Tunes Store and user interface redeveloped using WebKit, 6 Billionth song downloaded, 2 Billionth app downloaded, iTunes Versions 8.1 thru 9.0.2 released
2010 (iPad Launched)	iPhone 4, iTouch 4G, iPod Nano 6G iPod Shuffle 4G, iPad iOS 4.0, iPad iOS 3.2 support, support, iBook App and iBookstore introduced, Ping social network added, AirPlay added, Wi-Fi printing support, 10 Billionth song downloaded, iTunes U reported 300,000 downloads and 800 institutions, iTunes Versions 9.0.3 thru 10.1.1 released
2011	iPhone 4s, iPad 2, iOS 4.3 and iOS 5 support, Siri voice recognition, Apple TV 2G support, Mac App Store launched, iTunes in the Cloud launched, Wi-Fi Syncing, iCloud services launched, iTunes Match introduced, 18 Billionth App downloaded in October, $4 Billion in cumulative revenue sharing paid to developers, 500,000+ apps available in App Store, Over 200 million iOS users supported, iTunes Versions 10.1.2 thru 10.5.2 released
2012	iPad (3rd generation), Apple TV (3rd generation), iBook 2 App for iPad, iTunes U App, syncing support for iBooks 2 textbooks, iTunes Version 10.5.3 thru 10.6.1 released as of fiscal Q2.

Apple's experience provides insights into another element of elastic enterprises.

They have to operate as living organisms that interact and monitor customer activity, needs, wants and complaints and incorporate the experience of business ecosystem partners.

Apple is very careful to update software and make fixes, almost immediately, many times during the year as shown in the iTunes versioning history. In the process, features that fail are deleted and new functionality and features are added to all products through the year.

Finally let's talk economics.

Some analysts estimate that Apple has invested somewhere between $8 and $10 Billion to develop and implement their business platform since the iPod was introduced in 2001.

Some analysts have also estimated, based on a review of its published financial information and investments, that it costs more than $2 Billion per year to operate the business platform.

Although an enormous sum, the company has increased its quarterly profit from $8 Million in fiscal Q1 of 2003 to $13.06 Billion in fiscal Q1 of 2012 and put nearly $100 Billion in cash on the balance sheet since the iTunes business platform was introduced. Not a bad return on investment, particularly when you consider how that investment positions Apple for the future.

One additional note. Apple has been criticized for operating a closed business platform. In fact, from a business context, it is not.

Many companies and individuals transact with and contribute to the Apple platform. There are clear rules of engagement and transparent policies in any business platform but that does not mean the platform is closed.

A platform needs distinct rules of engagement for all participants, but it is truly open when anyone can join and participate— just like anyone can drive a vehicle on a highway assuming they have a license and obey the rules of the road.

One can quibble over the degree of openness, but we find that all business platforms must have rules of engagement to maintain order. A business platform without rules and limits becomes chaotic and rule setting is one of the most important processes a platform owner must design and manage.

Other Business Platforms in Action

Android is an almost identical concept to the Apple business platform and both compete in the mobile and advertising marketplace. With the introduction of Siri, the voice-directed assistant in the Apple business platform, it's possible that Apple will challenge Google's search business. But Android has proved very successful and represents a different approach to business platforms from that of its main competitor.

The Google Android business platform is more open.

Google has created a business platform and business ecosystem that includes a range of partners that manufacture different hardware devices. Each device runs the Android OS, in contrast to Apple who make both the hardware and the software for their own purposes only.

Google also allows its partners—software developers, hardware vendors and customers, to modify virtually any component of the Android software. Apple does not. Where Apple is in sole charge of the iPhone and iPad, Android involves hardware OEMs like Motorola Mobility (planned acquisition by Google in 2012 subject to regulatory approval), Samsung, LG and Sony Ericsson to mention a few (in total the OEM pool includes over 100 different devices using the Google Android OS on wide range of devices).[13]

These multiple vendors have agreed to a structure that effectively means they share the ecosystem of developers around the platform and to a lesser extent the ecosystem of customers for Android apps.

They are both collaborative and competitive around the devices and the optimization of apps and components for those devices.

It has been hugely successful in the sense that Android smartphones have been the fastest-growing product class in mobile smartphones over the period 2009–2011. Google claimed in December 2012 that Android activations were approach 700,000 per day,[14] another example of business acceleration from an elastic enterprise strategy.

In December of 2011, Google introduced a more controlled version of the Android OS, called Ice Cream Sandwich (Android OS 4.0) that requires vendors to install Android OS 4.0 in its released form without adding unique user interface components and behaviors.

This means that Google has added new rules for participation in the Google business ecosystem, and is an illustration of how a controlling company can and does change the playing field.

While the Android mobile OS and its related business platform receive the most press, the broader Google platform is much more diverse.

Google provides many different capabilities in its business platform including Google Maps, Google Apps, Google Voice, Google+ and many specialized programs and tools that developers can use and leverage for profit.

Like Apple, Google is also extremely active in developing its business platform and uses it as a major engine for strategy and operations.

Salesforce.com is another business platform player. It has expanded its business by turning its cloud-based customer relationship management (CRM) software into a business platform that now includes an entire marketplace of developers, third-party service providers and hardware providers, called Force.com.

Borrowing somewhat from Amazon, it became an open business platform for CRM software not just a software-as-a-service (SaaS) CRM product that it used to sell as a proprietary software offering.

In the process, Salesforce.com has been able to expand into a range of sub-markets that support different stages of the customer lifecycle. It has been able to enter new markets that provide other capabilities to businesses, such as its shared contacts database Jigsaw.

Not all examples are found in high tech.

USAA began operations in 1922 as an insurance company devoted to the risk management needs of U.S. military service men and women and their families. Today, the company is a fully integrated financial services firm that serves 7.7 million members that include non-military members as well.

In 2009, USAA wanted to create a new car-buying service for its customers and prospects. USAA envisioned a service that would provide detailed information on automobile features, deals, prices and trade-in values, real time loan origination services, preferred services via prequalified auto dealers and customers, and a mobile app to support customer inquiries.

In the past, like many companies, USAA would have developed an in-house custom system to deliver these services. That system would have run entirely in a USAA data center, requiring significant investment in new technology and software and considerable time for development. One more thing: USAA was not known as a car-buying resource in the general market when it started to think about its new auto-information service.

In 2009, USAA had the option of taking a business platform approach—an approach, as you will see, that provided it with new capabilities, credibility and the ability to extend its existing and new business rapidly into new markets with new customers.

Auto Circle, the brand name for the car buyer support service, is built on a business platform that USAA assembled through a combination of its existing information systems (i.e., financing, auto insurance) and a series of external platforms supplied by Vast (marketplace platform—research, search, inventory, matching, dealer connections), ZAG (auto transaction services), CARFAX (used car evaluation), Chrome Systems (auto dealer data platform) and the Apple mobile App platform and later Google Android.

The combined business platform offers an unprecedented level of service and convenience for the consumer. In fact, it established a new benchmark for auto buying services in the U.S. and possibly the world.

Remarkably, USAA was able to assemble Auto Circle in approximately a year. It did so by integrating existing platforms and by capitalizing on prior experience in developing iPhone apps. Auto Circle cost a fraction of what was required to set up a platform only a few years earlier because it could integrate third-party platforms and because of the growth of cloud-based services.

Launched in August of 2010,[15] by all measures, Auto Circle has been well received and customer satisfaction is high.

In the Fall of 2010, USAA saw a 77% increase in visits to the Auto Circle car-buying site, a 15% increase in auto loans, and a 23% year-to-year increase in automobiles sold.

Immediately after the introduction of the Auto Circle service, USAA used its experience in business platforms to introduce Home Circle. What Auto Circle did for car buyers, Home Circle does for real estate. It provides a range of price-related services for homebuyers and renters.

A platform strategy has clearly brought new agility to the enterprise and new options for business growth.

Three key lessons are worth noting in the USAA experience.

First, the recent growth in standardized interfaces and the entry of third-party providers of platform-based services enable any company interested in initiating a platform business to do it quickly and at a much lower cost than before.

Second, USAA built upon and transformed existing assets and core competence, using IT strategically without the waste of the past.

Third, in less than a year, USAA rapidly used its success with the Auto Circle platform business to move into an adjacent market with Home Circle, further leveraging its new competency, establishing a larger customer and partner ecosystem, and potentially disrupting existing players in the residential real estate industry.

We are seeing a small but growing rate of adoption of each of these capabilities in corporate America, Europe and China. And that's what underpins our optimism for the future. This is great business, cleanly, quickly executed.

Dynamic Two: Universal Connectors

In our earlier discussion of business platforms, we briefly touched on the idea of universal connectors. Today's software environment is snapped together and regularly repurposed because the connection points between systems and software are universally agreed.

This idea of automated interconnection is extremely important for business efficiency and scale. And as well as being evident at an architectural level it is also evident at the application level, the point where entrepreneurs create new business opportunities.

Think back to the early days of the World Wide Web. Suddenly a small symbol or acronym began appearing on websites, particularly those that hosted original content. The acronym was RSS and for many people it is still a mystery.

RSS is a powerful example of anonymized business relationships at work.

RSS stands for *really simple syndication*. It means that with a few mouse clicks, people can access your content in a stream, not just now but continuously whenever you publish.

When it arrived RSS was a new form of syndication, pulled, or subscribed to, initially by end-users. Eventually it would be used to create powerful new web content products like The Huffington Post, sold recently for in excess of $300 million.

RSS had a few other characteristics.

The content distributed via RSS was free. The server delivered the content at no cost to either the creator or reader. Both publishing and syndication were taking place free of charge. Yet there was also a contract there. Implicit in RSS is an agreement not to abuse copyright (often observed more in the breach than in the reality).

Secondly this was anonymous and easy to scale. The reader and creator would never meet each other and the creator might never know who the reader was. The relationship was anonymous even though they had a contract with each other.

But scale was very relevant to RSS—some authors had thousands upon thousands of readers pulling their RSS feeds, all effortlessly, at next to zero friction.

The contractual basis of the relationship was real and important. By taking the feed, the reader agreed not to misuse the information and the creator agreed to relax his or her copyright protection, knowing that the content would be used in some format.

And the proliferation of *free* work forced content creators to think how they should monetize their writing or what alternative value they could derive from having an interested, or engaged, audience. That in turn led to a very different view of how we build and treat reputation.

Gradually, the content feeds of bloggers and other content creators were incorporated into new products such as *The Huffington Post*, mentioned above.

A new class of company grew that used other people's content to create new information products, strictly speaking in contravention of copyright. But attitudes to copyright were changing. It was not such a big deal for most content creators to see their content used so long as they got reputational value from its use.

But look at what is happening here.

Just as the web represented a modular form of software at work, content too became modular, re-usable and widely re-used.

The product of a writer's imagination, the result of research, a product of painful reflection or whatever, it went into the pot and became a component that other people could and did use.

Distribution of ideas in some sense replaced the origination and production process, just as curation is now replacing creation.

Companies that stayed in the origination and production paradigm lost out—they could continue to create print-based content or they would create firewalls to try to charge for content. But very few such companies would find global audiences or benefit from the new economics of communications based around universal connectors.

RSS radically changed the content industry but it also created new social and economic structures typified by the new emphasis on public reputation in the social sphere and Google's Ad Sense in the economic. It is characteristic of universal connectors to transform what they touch.

This short history of content illustrates something vitally important. Universal connectors radically change the industries where they are introduced. The scope and impact of universal connectors is wide and profound. Universal connectors enable entirely new business platforms to be constructed and are transforming every industry.[16]

Universal connectors add flexibility to commercial arrangements and enhance the abilities of individuals, institutions and corporation to work together.

They move digital business beyond the proprietary systems used by most companies in the past. But they took a long time to develop.

Before universal connectors, each time a company had to connect dissimilar systems, or exchange data or do business electronically with another company, it had to modify each system and then create custom code to connect those systems. Maintaining all of these proprietary interfaces was time consuming and costly. Think back to before SMTP, the universal connector that lets people exchange emails across different systems. Before SMTP email was simply not universal.

Four broad categories of universal connectors now exist.

The first is the architectural standards that allow interconnection, described above. These are now expanding into identity, reducing online friction by creating one single sign on and transferring the focal point of business to the individual.

The second comprises content connectors like RSS, Twitter, SMS (i.e. texting), calendars, or instant messaging that enable virtually anyone to interconnect and exchange information.

The third category of universal connectors is used by programmers and software architects to make a plethora of dissimilar systems and technology interoperate. The latter category provides the capacity for entire systems to interconnect in a standardized way and interact productively under many conditions. These are usually called application programming interfaces (APIs).

Finally social networks take over many of the roles of universal connectors by integrating all communications within one platform (though this was eventually found by Facebook to be too limiting).

Examples of "professional" universal connectors include Application Programming Interfaces or APIs that connect businesses multilaterally, GPS, specialized sensors and telemetry automating machine-to-machine business models, as well as status and data streams that power collaboration.

And the professional category of universal connectors continues to develop. For example new types of universal connectors have developed around social network platforms like Facebook, LinkedIn and Google+.

Universal connectors propagated by social networks simplify the transfer of information about many of the events, communications and content broadly related to individuals and to companies doing social business. The sophistication and variety of the universal connectors available through social networking platforms has increased significantly in recent years and will continue to advance for some time.

APIs are a mystery to many people but they are part of the engine room of the new connected economy.

In the future, and the future is now, any device, appliance, machine or vehicle will have some form of universal connector so it can transact with other devices, individuals or organizations. For example, APIs are a major part of the so-called intelligent electricity grid, which will have millions of sensors, devices, switches and machines that all can intercommunicate, share data and be remotely operated.

Mashery, one of the three major players in the API management space, estimates that the average individual already has 147 connection points, from social networks, to mobile phones, to television sets, consoles and gaming platforms, to cars, home-mashups, even Lego pieces. Each of these represents multiple automated API transactions with a platform.

Mashery has already built APIs for Expedia, USA Today, Hoover's, Netflix, Klout, Dun and Bradstreet, The Guardian, New York Times, and BestBuy.

And of course the platforms interacting through these API calls can now be mashed together, as we see with USAA. The New York Times for example mashes data from its bestseller lists with the catalogue of the Collins Memorial Library, permitting customers to more easily locate NYT best sellers in the Collins catalogue.

Specialist API developers are now moving companies like Expedia to a hyper-channel future. For all of its existence Expedia was one company, one brand, serving one market. Then it opened an API for its affiliates and transformed itself into a multi-channel, hyper-local business delivered via local partners with particular local market knowledge and customer relationships. In other words via the API it was able to create and deliver mass differentiation.

APIs provide a deep level of technical sophistication for connecting dissimilar capabilities across companies, institutions and individuals. For example, APIs underlie the Cloud, the ability of mobile apps to interoperate across dissimilar networks, or for gamers to collaborate or compete across dissimilar personal computers, game consoles, and mobile devices. Caterpillar for example, led an industry-wide standards body to create an API to access and control heavy-duty earth moving equipment.

At the level of technical integration, APIs provide powerful mechanisms that enable diverse creators and dissimilar software producers using different software tools and architectures to connect their parts together.

They specify a uniform way of interfacing software functionality, which means all kinds of software can work together, even though it is not necessarily intended to. Developers and other specialized programmers have formed an entire sub-industry dedicated to creating APIs in response to the global demand to interconnect systems and technologies.

The development of universal connectors has practical implications. Apple, Google and USAA and other elastic enterprises would not have been able to develop and deploy business platforms and form business ecosystems without the emergence of universal connectors.

Here's a high level view of how universal connectors work. Universal connectors are built on standardized software architectures that specify rules for how connections will be made, how data must be packaged for transfer, requirements for security, and other details that enable coordination and timing.

For example, each individual app has to behave according to universal rules if it is function on Apple's iPhone and within Apple's various platforms, as well as the telecom carriers' platform and the specific apps' server platform that interacts with the app. The same is true for universal connectors for the Android OS or Window's mobile OS.

Each part must operate according to specifications packaged by the universal connectors. Because the specifications and operation of each universal connector are published and known, each party knows the rules and requirements for operating successfully with every other platform in the chain.

The social network provides another example of a dramatic transformation fostered by the universal connector paradigm.

Instead of seeking to connect via RSS or APIs, social networks like Facebook initially created large self-contained worlds where all the connections were internal to the platform.

At one stage it seemed as though social networks were trying to create their own mini-webs. Gradually they have opened up via APIs and now enable the interchange of many different types of content. User generated posts and content, and commercially created content from news organizations, advertisements, opinions, and so on. More recently, filmmakers and game producers others go inside Facebook to connect with audiences.

So universal connectors represent a new process for the enterprise.

They are born of a new philosophy. They support openness and speed. They allow business to be conducted in an increasingly frictionless and automated way so that costs are dramatically reduced, and the overhead of expansion is minimized. Connectors enable companies to work together via their systems, and to transfer and share data and link together with a minimum of effort.

For example, most major entertainment, broadcast and news organizations moved to a digital production model over the past decade. As a result, any news organization can acquire data feeds of news information in any format from any other news organization around the world in real time.

That information can be packaged with unique content, repackaged, distributed and offered back to the market. Companies like

Reuters, NBC Universal, Disney, Netflix, Al Jazeera, AOL, Google, BBC, CBC and virtually any other organization can connect their platforms to provide an infinite variety of news sources and services on demand.

Durable goods and heavy industrial manufacturers also use universal connectors. APIs allow Apple, Google, Android, Best Buy, Ford, Caterpillar, GE and many more companies to connect with and interact in an open way with tens to thousands of partners and their respective products.

The sensor network that powers GE's aircraft maintenance and performance improvement services rests on a variety of universal connectors that in turn connect to GE Aviation's communications partner, ARINC, or its worldwide network engine maintenance and overhaul providers and with customers, like Air Canada.[17] For example, GE Aviation's myEngines digital app delivers critical engine data to customer fleet managers on their smartphones or laptops as well as the desktop should they still need it.

The universal connector has another profound impact. As companies have gained experience in using APIs, they have also found that it becomes easier for them to serve micro-markets. This is integral also to the development of mobile computing and smartphones.

The App and its API's make the App a micromarketing tool. The breakthrough moment, Apple's App Store, showed that customers will self-segment markets at a very fine degree of granularity given the chance.

Each app in effect becomes a channel-creator, aggregating a customer base around a slightly differentiated product offering. Marketers working at the edge of technologically powered marketing now talk about these as hyper channels.

To do that though they need new channel partner strategies and these, in the elastic enterprise, emerge through business ecosystems rather than traditional bilateral partner contracts.

This is the world of connections and partnerships. APIs are a way to build connections. The unusual feature of them is that they help create partnerships at scale, and those partnerships take on the responsibility of creating and serving new micro-markets. That is the power of the universal connector.

Simply put universal connectors are universal—any person or any company can employ them. For example, Twitter has established a standardized format of short messaging that allows content creators and marketers to amplify their messages across the globe, in real time, at zero cost.

Millions of news feeds are shared with the ubiquitous RSS connector. Facebook, Google, Apple, Caterpillar, GE and many other companies have established standardized connectors to connect their business platforms, devices, equipment, and systems. And more industries and more companies will follow in their steps. The world of universal connectors will grow and in the process enable easier business partnering, scale and greater business flexibility.

Dynamic Three: The Cloud

The Cloud is the new *pervasive digital infrastructure*. It allows a frictionless business economy to grow and thrive. It provides unprecedented opportunities to innovate and to create wealth.

Among other things, the Cloud enables new services, for example, as we saw with USAA. The Cloud allows service developers to link business platforms from different enterprises into new services. Cloud also allows new service providers to set up shop with little capital cost.

Here is a definition:

"Cloud computing is a model for enabling convenient, on-demand network access to a shared pool of configurable computing resources (for example, networks, servers, storage, applications, and services) that can be rapidly provisioned and released with minimal management effort or service provider interaction."[18]

The Cloud is essentially an elastic infrastructure of storage, processing power and services that can be turned on and off like a tap, giving customers more of each when they need it, or less if demand peaks and goes into temporary decline. It is the ultimate business-driving machine. And it means companies can set up or scale new offerings at ultra-low cost relative to the past when they would need to make serious capital investments in those servers and software packages.

The Cloud means many things. But for our purposes, the Cloud is a common and public infrastructure that seamlessly enables business platforms and their globally scaled interactions. Cloud computing gives you the ability to expand and reduce resources according to your specific requirements. It's an enabler sometimes referred to as *elasticity and scalability*.

Because it is public and accessible it becomes a common elastic business infrastructure.

It also sets standards for the operation of so-called "private Clouds" that may be deployed for private or proprietary purposes.

And it can be deployed in a combination of public and private arrangements. For example, the U.S. Federal Government uses a combination of private Clouds and the public Cloud to deliver services, some that are secure and private and others that are also secure but share the Cloud with many other users.

Because the Cloud is shared, the cost of infrastructure investment and operation is also shared, and hence is less expensive than a private Cloud or an alternative closed and proprietary infrastructure.

The impact of the shared economics of Cloud infrastructure is not trivial. In most accounting systems Cloud will appear as an operational expenditure as distinct from a capital expenditure. It potentially releases a portion of CAPX (capital expenditures) that have formerly been spent on IT. Not only that. Because it releases CAPX and enables creativity in developing new services, based on

IT innovations, it is probably as responsible as the business platform for bringing IT back into the heart of the business.

Cloud also democratizes start-up and small company growth financing.

The low and elastic cost of the Cloud capacity means individuals and smaller companies can offer services to larger companies, based on a cloud infrastructure. Start-ups can get out there looking like a larger, accomplished company, equipped with the computing power of any rival.

That means a larger range of talent and services become available to everyone on this common elastic infrastructure. And in fact the effect of that has already been felt.

From 2010 onwards, large corporations began noticing their employees were using third-party applications to conduct some of their work. They might use Box.net for sharing documents with agencies or Huddle for online meetings or Basecamp for project management.

Each of these is a Cloud-based service. Each from its start-up phase onwards immediately began penetrating the large corporate software and services market.

Employees have embraced Cloud-based services—so much so that Box.net claimed in 2010 that it had over 75,000 corporations as clients, even though their client IT departments might not know it.

Cloud is that dramatic.

It not only allows smaller companies to create enterprise-grade services.

In addition, temporary business relationships are also more feasible. In the past, the cost of establishing a business relationship required a long payback period to make it feasible and productive. No longer!

Even ERP giant SAP is looking to exploit the capability of apps in the Cloud to establish immediate friction-free partnerships with its StreamWork project, a site that collates existing successful apps like Box.net.

SAP now offers a Cloud apps store, bringing the flexibility of apps to its installed client base. This is a huge change for old BIG ERP. Amazon too is collaborating with SAP to sell enterprise apps.

The shared economics of the Cloud contribute significantly to the friction-free elements of the new elastic approach to business formation, business models, and business operations. In the process it makes enterprises of all sizes more elastic.

Amazon.com is a powerful example of the Cloud in action.

For most of Amazon's history, the company utilized internally developed proprietary systems and infrastructure to conduct its business.

Its proprietary systems are legendary and contribute greatly to its success. Amazon knew early on that there was significant demand for its know-how. Amazon, after all, has unique experience of *scaling* online customer interaction.

In the early 2000s, Amazon began to make the systems that supported those highly scaled interactions available to other companies, for a fee.

One of the most public and dramatic examples was its agreement to support Target Stores. In 2002 Target's ecommerce infrastructure, customer relations and fulfillment were all served by Amazon. In fact Target.com was to all intents and purposes an Amazon operation, though Target had its own internet marketing team. By 2011 that relationship was over but prior to Target going it alone online, its Amazon-supported ecommerce arm enjoyed revenues of $1.3 billion in 2010, up from $1.2 billion in 2009 while its markets were still hit by recession.

Amazon had already supported Toys R Us and the late Borders online businesses prior to creating an end-to-end service for Target.[19]

In the process of developing these relationships, Amazon has continued to externalize its systems, to make them publicly available, and to enrich the range of services it offers.

Eventually, this led Amazon to create a fully-fledged Cloud infrastructure offer—that is, its servers, data storage, connectors, and most recently support services, based on a completely elastic pricing model.

In the process, it monetized the investment and operational costs of its systems, its infrastructure and its expertise that had traditionally been captive to Amazon alone.

Today, they are a player in the Cloud Services market and also make use of other company's Cloud offerings to power their growing non-retail businesses, particularly the e-reader business, Kindle. That's a powerful demonstration of the new imperative, and capacity, to select the best service provider for a specific business requirement.

More broadly, since almost everyone is connected to the Internet, it is now feasible to communicate with anyone on the planet and hence sell products and services that include anyone in any activity or venture. The advent of cheap mobile devices has accelerated the number of connections online and M2M commerce promises (or threatens) us with 1 trillion connected devices by 2015.

But the Cloud is what makes service creation and sales globally possible and efficient.

Because of the Cloud any company and any person now has potentially low cost access to financial markets, labor markets, retail markets, as well as formative and emerging micro-markets—anywhere, anytime.

As it develops, the Cloud will spawn further innovation as it connects more diverse parties and their ideas. For example, Rackspace and NASA initiated the OpenStack (www.openstack.org) consortium that now includes over 165 companies focused on creating a "massively scalable cloud operating system."

Other major players like IBM, Microsoft, CISCO, CA Technologies, AT&T, EMC, VMware, and HP, have already made significant investments and will continue to do so. Major IT Services companies like Accenture, Cognizant, TCS, Infosys, and Deloitte see the Cloud as a major vehicle for growth. We can also expect a continuing stream of new entrants across the Cloud space.

Additional international collaborative efforts will undoubtedly emerge over the next decade with expanding and interoperating business platforms and business ecosystems driving competition in the Cloud space.

Most importantly, the availability of the Cloud is one of the critical elements that supports the development and operation of the modern business ecosystem.

THE MAIN POINTS REVIEWED:

Business platforms are an important new competency for enterprises. They are as significant as the factory was to the industrial age. A company cannot contemplate the future without a platform strategy.

It is not always necessary to build a business platform but being able to assemble platforms is a core skill and a necessary enabler.

Business platforms have the added advantage of bringing IT and business functions back together and help continually align all functions around a common focus.

Universal connectors further enable elastic enterprises by automating key elements of many business processes and facilitating ultra-low cost business partnership development.

Finally Cloud is the new infrastructure that contributes massively to the creation of new business models on a pay-as-you-go basis.

These elements contribute three foundational dynamics to the elastic enterprise. But there are two more, business ecosystems and sapient leadership, explored in the next two chapters.

To get a feel for how prepared you might be for a business platform strategy ask:

1. To what extent are business platforms, universal connectors, and the Cloud operative in our firm?
2. Who are our natural communities?

3. What platforms do we currently use (ERP, social media monitoring, online communities) and what has been our experience?

4. Is our experience with platforms primarily technical in nature?

5. Is our experience closed or strictly proprietary in nature?

6. Can we see business platforms playing a role in our acquisition or merger strategies?

7. Do we regard our internal IT systems portfolio, IT investments or core systems as potential candidates for business platforms?

8. How might our business platforms support innovation?

9. How can we experiment with new business opportunities in the Cloud?

10. Can we combine innovation and venturing into a new platform and Cloud strategy, to gain experience in the new flexible architecture?

11. What is our universal connector strategy?

12. What ownership over process or customers can we share? Are we willing to share?

---

[1] Douglas Edwards, *I'm Feeling Lucky: The Confessions of Google Employee Number 59*. New York: Houghton Mifflin Harcourt Publishing Company, 2011.Mifflin Harcourt Publishing Company, 2011.

[2] See Don Tapscott, David Ticoll, and Alex Lowy in, *Digital Capital*, Harvard Business Press, 2000, for a discussion of extending existing products, services and value chains into b-webs or business webs See also Don Tapscott and Anthony Williams, *Wikinomics: How Mass Collaboration Changes Everything*, Portfolio/Penguin, New York, 2006 and also *Macrowikinomics: Rebooting Business and the World*, Portfolio/Penguin, New York, 2010.

[3] Nicholas G. Carr, *Does IT Matter? Information Technology and the Corrosion of Competitive Advantage*, Boston: Harvard Business School Press, 2004.

[4] http://www.w3.org/Consortium/mission

[5] http://www.oasis-open.org/

[6] http://tosca-open.org/

[7] Investments in the Cloud are accelerating. Even apparent critics, such as Larry Ellison, founder and Chairman of Oracle, are now making big bets through the acquisition of Cloud service providers. Microsoft, IBM, Apple, Amazon, Google, HP, Cisco and others have all added cloud offerings to their catalog of services. In our discussions with Jay M. Williams, currently Vice President of Engineering for Cloud Commons and Cloud Ecosystem at CA Technologies, he noted that current international standards bodies are working diligently to simplify access to the Cloud.

[8] The business platforms used by elastic enterprises are designed and constructed to be extensible. In this sense they have the apparatus to allow external partners and collaborators to join the business platform. Apple's iPhone and iPad business platforms, as well as Google's Android are good examples. The use of platforms in business is not new. But, prior platforms tended to be proprietary in nature and relatively closed in membership. For an excellent analysis of early platform-based competition in the high technology industry see Annabelle Gawer and Michael A. Cusamano, *Platform Leadership: How Intel, Microsoft, and Cisco Drive Industry Innovation*, Harvard Business School Press, Boston MA, 2002. See also Caroline Calklins and John Sviokla's work on the advantages of business platforms in M&A, "Mergers and Acquisitions in the Age of Business Platforms," Insight Series, Diamond Management & Technology Consultants, Chicago, IL, 2006. We have also discussed elsewhere the evolution of platforms in business, see Nicholas Vitalari and Laura Carrillo, *Building a Platform for Business Growth: Enabling Connection, Collaboration and Innovation*, nGenera Research Report, 2009.

[9] Philip Elmer DeWitt, "Transcript: Apple CEO Tim Cook at Goldman Sachs," Fortune, February 15, 2012, http://tech.fortune.cnn.com/2012/02/15/transcript-apple-ceo-tim-cook-at-goldman-sachs/

[10] The concept of strong and weak interpersonal relationships has become a fundamental concept in the science and analysis of social networks and online communities. Mark Grannovetter developed the concept in a now classic paper in "The Strength of Weak Ties," *The American Journal of Sociology* Vol. 78, No. 6, pp. 1360–1380, and later in 1983 in "The Strength of Weak Ties: A Network Theory Revisited," Sociological Theory, Vol. 1, pp. 201–233.

[11] When Steve Jobs returned to Apple, he brought with him, Avie Tevanean from NeXT who was one of the principles in the Mach OS research project at Carnegie Melon University. Mach was an attempt to build more flexibility into the core

kernel of the Unix operating system to facilitate among other things more complex inter-process communication to support distributed OS and distributed computing systems. Tevanean became Senior Vice President of Software Engineering at Apple from 1997–2003 and then assumed duties as Chief Technology Officer at Apple from 2003–2006.

[12] Mark McClusky, The Nike Experiment: How the Shoe Giant Unleashed the Power of Personal Metrics, *Wired Magazine*, 17.07, June 22, 2009, http://www.wired.com/medtech/health/magazine/17-07/lbnp_nike?currentPage=all

[13] Wikipedia provide an unaudited list of Android device manufacturers and devices the provides a sense of the equipment partners, see http://en.wikipedia.org/wiki/Comparison_of_Android_devices

[14] Matt Brian, "Google Announces 3.7m Android Activations over the Christmas Weekend," TNW, December 28, 2011, http://thenextweb.com/google/2011/12/28/google-announces-3-7m-android-activations-over-the-christmas-weekend/

[15] see https://www.usaa.com/inet/ent_blogs/Blogs?action=blogpost&blogkey=newsroom&postkey=autocircle_homecircle_new

[16] While beyond the scope of this book, it does not take much investigation to find major examples of technical white papers in virtually any industry discussing universal connectors. While each industry has its nomenclature and standard specifications, specialized universal connectors are essential for battlefield systems, drone operations, telemedicine, high speed medical imaging, publishing, digital studios in media production, intelligent equipment use in agriculture and farming, real-time trading platforms, intelligent energy grids, and real time video feeds.

[17] http://www.geaviation.com/aboutgeae/presscenter/services/services_20110412a.html

[18] Peter Mell and Timothy Grance, *The NIST Definition of Cloud Computing: Recommendations of the National Institute of Standards and Technology*, Special Publication 800-145, National Institute of Standards and Technology, U.S. Department of Commerce, Washington, D.C. September 2011.

[19] See Tony Kontzer, Amazon's E-Commerce Technology is On Target, Information Week 19th August 2002

CHAPTER 4
PEOPLE UNLIMITED

Dynamic Four: Business Ecosystems

In the last chapter, we introduced the five dynamics of the elastic enterprise and delved into the detail of the first three. In this chapter, we focus on the business ecosystem and sapient leadership.

Ecosystems are agglomerations of people and companies that work together through a business platform without the benefit of multilateral contracts. They represent an unprecedented unleashing of talent and innovative capacity, when done right.

Think of the many interlocking communities around Google's apps products and Android's mobility products. Google's Map application and architecture have drawn together a powerful ecosystem of developers, cartographers, spatial and data scientists, groups that might not otherwise have interacted. Google has created fertile cross-disciplinary relationships. And in Android, Google stimulates collaboration between handset OEMs, building important partnerships between competitors and their supply chains. Automotive companies have also congregated around Google's Map application and its architecture.

An enterprise empowered with a business ecosystem no longer operates alone, but rather in a league with thousands, hundreds of thousands or millions of quasi-partners.

Business ecosystems power the scope, scale and versatility of the elastic enterprise. Empowered by the three dynamics of business platforms, universal connectors and the Cloud, business ecosystems add a fourth dimension of structure that radically extends the boundaries of the corporation.

The business ecosystem enables an enterprise to service a range of diverse markets and customer preferences in conjunction with a virtually inexhaustible community of partners, each with its own means of production, all motivated by common goals of creativity and wealth creation.

Precursors to the Business Ecosystem

Business is primarily about the organization of resources to meet market demand. In the past, that meant being able to source raw materials, components and people to deploy against fairly predictable assumptions about market demand. Business ecosystems are a new system for resource allocation—or resource attraction. They are essential for very obvious reasons.

What we could safely assume about markets in the past, we can no longer project into the future, for all the reasons we've touched on in previous chapters.

Business ecosystems are replacing structured demand and the structured supply chains that we were formerly able to build into our assumptions about how markets functioned.

What is changing?

Markets used to be chain-like, consisting of several interlocking parts in a linear relationship. A typical chain had a sequence as follows: raw material sourcing, component sourcing, assembly, marketing, sales, and customer relationship management. This chain model is now defunct.

The new business ecosystem and its behavior, though, is not yet as clear as the old chain model used to be. It's not that we can't describe business ecosystems. The problem is that the nature of ecosystems is also changing. In the not-so-distant past, we could identify a business ecosystem and point to its advantages with relative ease.

The old ecosystem was an actor in the traditional chain of business, limited to a defined set of members and participants.

In his classic book, The Visible Hand, business historian Alfred Chandler argued that the rise of effective hierarchies and professional management in the late 1800s and 1900s led to the efficiencies of the modern corporation, specifically their ability to grow and manage scale.[1]

His thesis aptly describes the strategy and structure of the traditional global industrial corporation. But hierarchies and professional management are not sufficient to describe the strategy and structure of the elastic enterprise. There are other "visible hands" at work in the elastic enterprise. Namely, the business ecosystem.

Precursors to the business ecosystem include well-known companies or business networks like the Japanese keiretsu (e.g., Mitsubishi, Mitsui, Toyota), the Chinese huaren gongsi (e.g., Haier) and the Korean chaebol (e.g., Samsung, Daewoo), as well as complex supply chains that support particular industries.

The keiretsu, huaren gongsi, and chaebol organizations bring together individual companies to pool necessary capital investment and amass the scale required to compete in global markets.

Complex supply chains in the global automotive, global aerospace or global electronics industries are also types of business networks that support large scale inbound and outbound logistics.

However, these types of business networks tend to be insular, based on multilateral contracts or, at best, are limited to preferred or qualified vendors. Frequently, membership also involves interlocking directorates, joint ventures or even formal legal structures, and in some cases, familial structures.

For example, software giant Microsoft ascended to an incredible position of power and influence in enterprise software because it grew and managed a highly disciplined "old style" ecosystem.

At its peak, that ecosystem comprised over 75,000 partners, or Value Added Resellers (VARs) and Independent Software Vendors, (ISVs).

Each of the VARs/ISVs in the ecosystem had dual roles.

The first was to become expert in Microsoft software technologies such as .NET or SharePoint.

That expertise had to be sufficient to customize Microsoft technologies for existing and potential customers and/or to propose business solutions to those customers and prospects.

The second important role was to sell the benefits of Microsoft technologies in a competitive market, in effect to grow Microsoft's customer base.

That gave Microsoft a huge ecosystem to sell on its behalf and was very much in the tradition of the value chain model of business.

"Modern" business ecosystems are quite different.

Sure, there are benefits that accrue to Apple through having 300,000 apps developers, but these developers are entirely separate businesses with their own diverse relationships, channels, contracts and indeed alternative ecosystems that they participate in. This is an entirely new arrangement.

The reason we refer to it as a business ecosystem is that it has a dynamic all of its own. Its members are neither wholly nor partially dependent upon Apple or any other cornerstone company or platform owner.

A business ecosystem is a more varied entity. In essence, it is a critical part of a new more elastic operating system, a new way to organize and allocate resources. In contrast to previous business communities, the new ecosystem members totally own their own means of production and operate independently of the business ecosystem as well as being a member of it.

A business ecosystem can be built around a common product or category of products. For example, the Apple business ecosystem is built around the Apple iPod, iPhone and iPad and the Apple IOS operating system.

Or it can be an ecosystem for labor and talent, combining freelance, sub-contract, open innovation, crowdsourced, outsourced and other labor and talent formats. Labor ecosystems also rely increasingly on platforms, such as open innovation platforms or crowdsourced platforms like Mechanical Turk.

Finally, we see the growing presence of customer ecosystems, also based around platforms, like YouTube and Flickr.

The lifeblood of these companies circulates around the many relationships they need to foster in order to grow. They operate in a highly competitive business environment and one that is constantly shifting.

There are dependent relationships out there that hark back to the old ecosystem model.

For example on the Facebook platform, the games company Zynga is largely dependent on Facebook for its revenues and growth. Of late Zynga has been trying to take its casual gaming products outside the Facebook platform.

In contrast, on the Apple and Android platforms companies might have only fleeting relationships and low revenues from any one of these. They need to develop multiple lives across multiple ecosystems.

Microsoft's Independent Software Vendors, on the other hand, carried a badge saying *Microsoft Approved, or Microsoft Gold Partner,* after paying for Microsoft training. That relationship had depth and a sense of exclusivity.

In today's more universal web world, developers get a software development kit in exchange for $99, and then get on with developing an app. In place of joint marketing agreements between a cornerstone company and a VAR or ISV, developers sell in a largely anonymous store in competition with each other.

They own their product and can adapt it for any other App Store. Their participation is a commitment but not a partnership. For example many of the apps available on the Apple App Store are now also available on the Android platform.

Yet, they are still an Apple resource, a resource that Apple has organized for its own strategic needs. And, indeed, this form of free-flowing ecosystem is now evident around Microsoft with a small number of SharePoint App Stores opening during 2010 and 2011 so that developers can share, sell and buy SharePoint functionality, with or without Microsoft's involvement.

The business ecosystem is not confined to the immediate platform and customer relationships. Elastic enterprises also build contingent labor pools and they are large users of outsourced manufacture. This is not unique to elastic enterprises but it is essential to their success. Elasticity tends to incorporate all resource allocation decisions.

A company that takes an elastic view of resources needs to understand its ecosystem and the overlapping ecosystems around it, because all of these bring resource benefits—for example, in terms of making software components available, making lower cost labor available or being able to access talent anywhere, anytime, or giving the enterprise rapid access to innovations.

The Components of a Business Ecosystem

Business ecosystems are assembled from many components. But as we pointed out in the last chapter the business platform and the business ecosystem are co-dependent (see Figure 3.3). This synergistic relationship between the modern business ecosystem and the business platform bares some similarity to natural ecosystems.

Natural ecosystems conform to a power law that allows them to grow without incurring a disproportionately large overhead expense in terms of energy.

But they are also prone to a natural selection process, with weaker entities being squeezed out as stronger entities prove their vitality

Our purpose here is to highlight some of the other critical components to consider: the cornerstone company, the information infrastructure, outsourced manufacture, contingent labor pools, outsourced innovation, crowdsourcing and customer ecosystems.

The cornerstone company.

We have discussed business platform at length, but more must be said of the essential role of the cornerstone company.

The cornerstone company leads, attracts and orchestrates, provides many or all of the components of the business platform, and usually is an industry leader and the sponsoring enterprise (e.g., Apple, Amazon, Mozilla).

The cornerstone company assures the economic viability and growth of the business ecosystem and business platform and uses its market credibility to attract resources such as talent to the business ecosystem.

A cornerstone company does not take any responsibility for training or supporting its members directly. They are left to sink or swim, by and large, though the cornerstone company will provide general support to **ALL** members, roughly equally and transparently.

That, by the way, underlines an important point of successful ecosystems: transparency and equality.

The level of support given by the cornerstone company varies. It can be just a software developer kit, and a self-service developer community. That in fact is the norm. In cases like The Guardian, however, the cornerstone company becomes involved as a coach and investor. In a case like Expedia, the cornerstone company provides significant collateral support to members of its new API/affiliate community.

There is a risk-reward calculation to be made about what works, at what price, and with what levels of control. In general as we said before, ecosystems tend to function in a very transparent way with a notable degree of equality.

The information infrastructure.

Ecosystems also typically include the information infrastructure around a market: blogs, news organizations, influencers, conferences.

There is a tendency to neglect this part of the ecosystem at the planning stage. But the information infrastructure is absolutely vital to success. It cannot be controlled by old public relations methods. We'll touch later on how skilled leaders influence the information part of the ecosystem.

Outsourced manufacture.

The ecosystem also consists of large-scale outsourcing. Foxconn, the Chinese component manufacturer, specializes in a rarefied form of production and assembly coupled with huge capital investment in factories that produce components at close to the minimum possible price. Apple, Amazon and many other companies take advantage of that, and it is essential to making the whole package of device and apps work.

And, of course, many companies utilize similar processes for higher value-added work such as software design and coding.

Contingent labor pools.

The development of contingent talent pools in India, Russia, Eastern Europe, Brazil and China means that there is barely a start-up in Europe or the U.S. that does not have a contingent workforce offshore.

Modern ecosystems are not unique in making use of contingent labor pools but we shouldn't shy away from acknowledging that their success is tied up in low cost labor as well as the independent talent pool.

Outsourcing innovation.

The use of elastic resources as we go forward will go further—much further—than contingent workforces.

Outsourcing has been around for twenty or more years. Like so many parts of the economy it too is changing shape.

The next phase of outsourcing includes the outsourcing of innovation tasks—forging the breakthrough changes in product or process offshore, on behalf of a client company.

The outsourcing of innovation is a service that leading suppliers such as Cognizant are finding is very much in demand from clients as they seek ways to understand the new business environment. Companies like Innocentive and Nine Sigma meanwhile offer to source highly specialized talent on a "challenge" basis, that is issuing public and sometimes closed challenges to members of the public or to select groups of specialists.

Crowdsourcing.

Simultaneously, a new phase of outsourcing has evolved: crowdsourcing.[2] Crowdsourcing can function in creative environments, and is sometimes the baseline for open innovation projects. But it can also function in routine processes.

We are about to witness the rapid growth of crowdsourced routine tasks. Amazon's Mechanical Turk, the ability to break work processes down to ever-smaller units and then to outsource these to very low wage economies like Africa[3] via game-centric or mobile text-based tasks, is finally taking off.

Customer ecosystems.

On the customer side of the business ecosystem, change is just as rapid. In a 2011 study of the British economy, the MIT open innovation theorist Eric Von Hippel noted that consumers spend twice as much as firms on improving, changing or innovating products.[4] Enterprise leaders who see a customer where they might more profitably see a partner have long overlooked this creative capacity.

The growth of customer ecosystems or the integration of customers into business ecosystems has gone furthest in the print and broadcast media.

In print, readers have always had the option of sending in letters to the editor. Today, their comments on newspaper web sites are integral to many of the stories, the number of comments signaling, for example, the importance of a topic to other readers.

The advent of cheap videophones has deepened and broadened customer involvement in media. American broadcaster CNN, however, has gone much further than most with its iReport service, a dedicated channel for viewers to send in news content.

As of the time of writing, CNN has announced its intention to convert iReport to a social network, which will more fully blur the line between viewer, reader and producer. CNN has also expanded its commitment to support multiple end-user devices that now include a range of traditional screens and mobile devices.

On web sites like YouTube and Flickr, the integration of the customer and viewer is already complete.

What might be lacking in these cases are tools that allow viewers to become more actively involved in promoting content and building business opportunity from it. Neither YouTube nor Flickr have been able reframe the customer's role sufficiently, even though each "owns" a truly significant piece of business history in their huge customer ecosystem platforms.

Neither has embarked on a critical reframing of their relationship with the customer. Some newer entrants, such as SmugMug, Instagram (acquired by Facebook) and Vimeo, may signal the next phase of content ecosystems and the addition of community elements with social networking, professional tools and commerce engines that let customers/viewers rate, co-create and sell content.

A business has to take advantage of these trends—its role is to organize and allocate resources effectively. The new labor force, the human element of resource allocation, in effect involves all these ecosystem choices: developers, freelance designers and marketers, the outsourced standardized tasks, outsourced innovation, contingent workforces and game-centric labor.

Today's leaders have to step up and reframe the notion of business around their ecosystem activities. We can no longer frame the world as divided between business and customer, corporation and individual, or supplier and producer, nor see their own organizations as in any sense a self-contained unit. Elasticity requires new management thinking and new disciplines.

Operating an Ecosystem

When it comes to operating a business ecosystem, the prime directive is to assure it vibrancy and sustainability. A business ecosystem also depends on mutual interdependence and mutual benefit for all partners and members. In complex business ecosystems, like Apple, Google, Facebook or Amazon, each participating entity has a constellation of different objectives ranging from financial gain, building brand awareness and equity, to serving a noble purpose.

However, in addition to the having a strong cornerstone company, several other features create a productive environment for a successful business ecosystem:

Purpose. Successful business ecosystems are marked by some moral or higher purpose. They can be great cash generators but still be purpose-driven. Apple's ease-of-use design is part of a movement to change how computing is done, for example.

Rules of the road to guide the business ecosystem partners, members and contributors in what they can and can't do. Rules and policies, if properly designed can assure everyone gets a fair deal.

Excellent **ingest facilities and tools**—for example, an SDK and mechanisms for the ecosystem to contribute that is both highly formalized and extremely easy to use.

A geographically and **culturally diverse set of contributors acting as peers** (companies, individuals, entities, institutions), often virtually connected, that voluntarily come together for mutual benefit and gain.

Diverse incentives and rewards—each contributor expects an economic return for its effort, though we are seeing non-financial rewards play a bigger part in ecosystems like that around the open source browser Mozilla and in other areas of the open source movement, and in content production.

A **marketplace** of buyers and sellers.

A big question that is often overlooked is the purpose of the business ecosystem. It is true that many successful business ecosystems exist for profit but, as in other areas of the changing business world, profit is not everything. The implicit purpose of the business ecosystem might indeed be financial but it is very likely to be much larger than that.

Purpose is a key motivation in the new business climate.

Often purpose (e.g., how noble the purpose, how meaningful, how revolutionary) is a prime motivation to participate in an ecosystem. It is also the basis of what makes a business ecosystem sustainable. Purpose provides movement. If it becomes "a movement," then the business ecosystem has captured the minds and hearts of its participants and is also likely to catch the attention of people in other communities and ecosystems as well.

It is thought, for example, that relatively few apps in Apple's App Store actually make a profit. That's in part because many are now adjuncts to corporate marketing campaigns—the American Airlines app makes it easier to book on American via the iPhone and is one of many thousands of these market-orientated apps.

Apple succeeded in part, though, because it evoked the sense of a giant movement to a different way of doing business, one that gave the "little guys" a chance.

Android succeeds because it is a global movement to reduce the cost of mobile communications.

The ultimate purpose of the modern ecosystem has to combine diverse economic, reputational and moral objectives. But even so, we cannot lose sight of how broadly "economic value" is now interpreted.

In the Forbes.com ecosystem of writers, many are not paid at all but they do see reputational benefits that might bring them rewards outside the ecosystem.

At the other extreme, participants in the Mozilla marketing ecosystem contribute largely for reputational gains with next to no opportunity for earnings. Most open source ecosystems still rely on 25–50% of their participants contributing without cash rewards.[5]

As a consequence, the platform leader and orchestrator must invest, facilitate and establish rules to support the business platform and ecosystem in ways that talk to a variety of human motivations.

Healthy business ecosystems spell out the covenants and conditions for membership and participation as well as the rewards. In other words, successful business ecosystems run on well-designed rules of the road, which head off confusion. Take a look at the Mozilla marketing community as an example. And they are not afraid of doing that in moral tones.

Business ecosystems have rules laid down by a leader. Those rules can be about the types of permissible applications, the application ingest process, the association with the lead company or the cost of the SDK.

Not all the partners in the business ecosystem may agree with the rules of membership, but unanimity is not necessary. Developers and Apple have disagreed over several key issues, not least in the first instance the availability of an SDK, and latterly over the use of Flash. But these are necessary conflicts. They illustrate a real dynamic rather than a hierarchical relationship.

Good business platforms provide ample opportunity for business ecosystem partners to voice issues, discontent or suggestions. Leaders have to remain open to persuasion. Ecosystems are ultimately self-sufficient communities with a high degree of internal volition. They are peer groups and see themselves as peers of the lead company's own leadership team. They too are businesses and want respect shown for their business objectives.

Crucially there is no prejudice in these ecosystems. A peer is truly an equal and no potential member is discriminated against on the grounds of geography, culture, color, age (the youngest App Store developer is 12 years old), or gender.

The result of careful curation of purpose and respect is a group of partners that are well acquainted with operational conventions for doing business within the ecosystem, even if they don't like all of those conventions.[6] And a partner base that is motivated.

The leader must also lay the reputational groundwork for this ecosystem. Ecosystems have to aspire to lead their industry. It is the role of the orchestrator to make sure this happens. The orchestrator is in charge of the ecosystems amplification tools, the way that reputation gets established and built.

An important part of this process in future will revolve around curating the relationship between customers and developers, for example, ensuring that privacy concerns are properly managed.

Getting these parts of the formula right make it more likely that a company will function as an attractor of resources and the privacy issue shows that what is needed to remain attractive changes over time.

Even sharp management teams can get it wrong.

Google took time to establish its Android community and risked losing the developer community before both parties (Google and the developers) began to forge an understanding of the real objectives of Android.

For the first two years of its life, it was overshadowed by the vast buzz around the iPhone. Its attraction quotient was inadequate for this competitive situation.

In fact, when the first Android phone was launched in 2008, Apple's iPhone still enjoyed 12 times more online references (blog posts, tweets, comments, news stories) than Android, an imbalance that took two more years to rectify as the Android ecosystem grew and, essentially, became more vocal, and more capable of growing an information infrastructure.

Crucially, the platform leader needs both to interpret and lead—to interpret the motivation of potential participants and to lead on issues where consensus and business conditions might be misaligned. But it also needs to maintain a sense of market leadership so that the participants feel they are with the number one platform in their area. Contributing to the number two platform has few reputational benefits.

In mobile telephony, Nokia attempted to start and grow an ecosystem around its Symbian operating system—similar to Android. After a year, the Symbian developer platform, Horizon, had just 65 apps on it. It soon became a reputational liability.

Within two years Android by way of contrast was well on the way to closing the reputational gap with the iPhone (the amplification gap decreased to 3:1 over this period). Google began to master the information amplification war and to successfully parlay Android as a leader with objectives that differed from Apple's.

To compete effectively in diverse and highly interconnected global economies, all companies must either lead and/or be part of one or more business ecosystem.

They must create, join and participate because very few enterprises will sit at the apex of their own global ecosystem like a feudal overlord. Ecosystem leadership requires a new way of looking at business and a new participatory, collaborative mindset.

The absence of those qualities gives rise to the kinds of friction and litigation that we are now seeing in the software patent trolls. Clearly, culture change is paramount. But the fifth dynamic, leadership, is undergoing the most radical change of all.

Dynamic Five: Sapient Leadership

When Steve Jobs embarked on the reconstruction and turnaround of Apple Computer in 1997, his management style was largely formed through three experiences: the founding and early development of Apple; the founding and operation of NeXT Computer, his first post-Apple project; and the strategic guidance of Pixar, the pioneering digital animation studio.

In each situation, he was massively successful.

And each experience contributed to his leadership approach and style. But the most significant change took place on his return and transformation of Apple. However, since the introduction of the iPod in 2001, Steve Jobs has made remarkable and public changes in his management style that have largely gone unnoticed. Over the last decade of his life Jobs reframed his management style as he reframed the company, its competencies and objectives.

He came to embody the characteristics of a leader who understands how to attract, orchestrate, manage and operate the resources that Apple needed.

He added these crucial new leadership skills to his already formidable leadership repertoire.

The financial results of Apple and its amazing share price performance put him among, if not at the top of, the most celebrated business leaders of the last 100 years. Steve Jobs epitomizes the sapient leader.

Critical to this transformation is a notion that Jobs used on March 2, 2011, introducing the iPad 2:

> It's in Apple's DNA that technology alone is not enough—
> it's technology married with liberal arts, married with the
> humanities, that yields us the results that make our heart
> sing.

This idea that business has to marry different disciplines is significant because the sapient leader has one capacity above all others: the ability to reframe the conceptual world of the business, indeed of business in general.

Cognitive reframing is the first skill of the sapient leader. And Steve Jobs is a consummate re-framer. For a decade he reframed Apple from a computing to a telephony and a media company and more.

There are other sapient leadership skills, and we'll come to them in the next chapter.

Reframing however is a concept we want to introduce before we go on to discuss leadership in detail.

When humans encounter change, they typically resist it.

That's because much of what we experience as change requires a significant cognitive shift that we feel as a form of psychic pain. For some the associated anxiety can generate physical discomfort.

Humans do not change their minds easily, they do not opt for change lightly. And when they need to change it is often because a leader has successfully reframed a potentially threatening situation into something altogether more dynamic and positive.

This is the act of cognitive reframing.

The reason we introduced Jobs again at this stage is that experience seems to have fitted him out to reframe the environment around him.

One source of his own personal inspiration was his early induction into typography.

His career was significantly influenced by a one-semester course in typography while at Reed College. Later, in fact as late as 2005, Jobs recounted that experience and why he had designed beautiful typography into the first Mac.

> When we were designing the first Macintosh computer, it all came back to me. And we designed it all into the Mac. It was the first computer with beautiful typography. If I had never dropped in on that single course in college, the Mac would have never had multiple typefaces or proportionally spaced

fonts. And since Windows just copied the Mac, it's likely that no personal computer would have them.[7]

What Tim Carmody points out when quoting this from Jobs's 2005 Stanford commencement speech is that in renewing Apple from 1997 onwards, Jobs converted the former technology company into a media company.

That reframe took Apple beyond typography deep into the creative aspects of the screen and human interaction.

If you had listened to the computing industry in the early 1990s the message was all about Moore's Law, the doubling of processing power every 18 months. Jobs meanwhile set off on a different journey. Jobs peers were still selling Wintel PCs as essentially a power feature.

He went in search of advantage in the convergence of communications' technologies and the liberal arts—music and video—through iTunes and the iPod.

Eventually, he exploited the combination of technological and artistic creativity in apps.

And he was on top of the convergence of computing and mobile communications from a very early stage with the iPhone.

Jobs successes rest partly on these convergence factors, the merging of different markets. But they illustrate an important new role of leaders. At each stage he had to reframe the cognitive environment for his staff, ecosystem and the information infrastructure around him. He had to persuade people to see these transitions as normal, natural and highly beneficial.

That reframing capability is what leaders need in the modern economy. It is a highly conceptual role, one that also requires significant levels of peer respect and persuasive personal interaction because at every reframe a leader has to take not only employees but also the peer ecosystem along with him or her.

The *first* significant cognitive reframe Jobs achieved at Apple was to introduce the liberal arts as a key driver of its business model. It would not just make computers it would make devices that serve the arts (the iPod), it would sell artistic products like music, and it would place renewed emphasis on the integral beauty of its devices.

The *second* significant cognitive reframe was in the business model. Apple converted itself from a seller of devices to a reseller of music.

In the process, it came into contact with an entirely different ecosystem and managed its relationships with the creative industry with aplomb. While the Macintosh was already well established in the creative arts and film communities, this new thrust opened Apple to additional business ecosystems and players.

The *third* major reframe was to create a new way of dealing with mobile phone networks, away from the traditional network as dominant partner model when Nokia ruled the mobile device space. In Apple's relationships with networks it appears to have secured a proportion of mobile traffic revenue, a feat never attempted by Nokia, as well as forcing the operators to sell extended contracts to customers along with the iPhone.

The *fourth* major reframe was of course the iPhone itself and then the iPad and the introduction of an independent lite-software app strategy. An important sub-element of the cognitive reframing story for Apple is important. As Steve Jobs interacted more and more with the iPhone business ecosystem, he also altered his management style. He became more flexible and accommodating.

Apple shared more revenue with its developers than it had in the past. Apple became much more public in sharing its plans for its SDK, or developers' toolkit. And Apple became much more responsive to correcting problems or adding new features to its IOS, based on suggestions from its developer community.

From 2008 to 2011, Steve Jobs himself also became more vocal and active in selling Apple's vision to its business ecosystem and its policies.

All of these elements illustrate just how much reframing and change Jobs made in Apple's approach to business and also in his own personal management style—changes that became increasingly necessary when operating with a global business platform and diverse business ecosystem.

Why call these cognitive reframes?

The reality of these moves is that they involved major cognitive changes for Jobs, his staff and the wider ecosystem. He had to take his people and his peers on several significant radical adjacency moves.

There is no such thing as an easy adjacency move.

Companies do not move with ease from one product set to another. They often struggle to make even minor moves into new markets.

Adjacencies, as these moves are known, are a major source of business failure. Part of the reason for that is that many corporations function through deep-seated cognitive assumptions that riff through a corporate culture and make alternative forms of behavior extremely difficult for employees, executives, investors or partners to countenance.

As Apple ascended into the smartphone sector it had to compete against a deeply embedded market leader, Nokia. In 2007 at the time of the iPhone launch Nokia was totally dominant in mobile devices, selling approximately half a billion devices a year. Apple's entry coincided with a dramatic long-term descent for Nokia, because Apple reframed what mobile phones were for in western culture, what they could do, how they should look, how easy they were to use.

The reason for Nokia's decline was not simply that Apple had outsmarted Nokia. Nokia was not able to do the cognitive reframe. It tried to launch an App Store (Ovi) but it found great difficulty in telling itself and its customers a new story about Nokia as a services provider. People knew Nokia devices but its services story sounded hollow, and its launch of a global platform simultaneously in all of its major markets was sheer hubris. Nokia could only tell a story about its own leadership. It could not reframe.

Because it could not reframe, Nokia remained the Nokia everyone knew—the largest mobile device maker in the world and the best mobile hardware engineering firm in the world. But perhaps Nokia was not the best at design or user-interaction or at converting its developer community into an ecosystem. Its attraction skills were founded in the past on the size of its market but the rules changed when Apple reframed phone design.

In everything it did, and whatever its executives tried to say or do, Nokia remained the Nokia of the 1990s, in a world that Apple has shifted on its axis.

Nokia proclaimed that its Ovi Store would be the biggest and best in the world. It launched the Ovi Store simultaneously in 35 countries, 10 months after Apple launched the App Store. But Nokia's ambition and arrogance was catastrophic.

The platform was not well enough developed to support a global launch and criticism inevitably came fast and very furious. Dated May 26, 2009, the influential tech web site TechCrunch announced: Nokia Ovi Store Launch Is A Complete Disaster.

Nokia's barely legible, small-screen devices were shown up by Apple's ultra-sleek iPhone interface.

Nokia had an option to join the new Android open source operating system community and accelerate its route to cleaner, more usable interfaces. But the world's biggest mobile device maker refused to use an operating system that was not its own, even though Google's Android soon became the fastest growing of all mobile operating systems.

In an act of what many view as a capitulation, Nokia eventually signed a partnership with Microsoft, another company with a large and big history. Nokia is still struggling. It is still Nokia. It has not reframed by partnering with Microsoft even though its newer devices are more attractive than the old.

The point about the cognitive reframe is that leaders can be as bright as a button but unless they can bring an organization and an ecosystem along with them, unless they can inspire, and engage many thousands of people to change perceptions, and do the reframe with them, then strategy will hit a wall.

Cisco is another example of a company struggling to cognitively reframe. It has cultivated many different business ecosystems. It has invested in business platforms and business portals with suppliers and service providers. And it has developer communities.

But upon closer examination, Cisco's attempts to reinvent itself is disconnected and fragmented.

It attempted a major adjacency move through the acquisition of the Flip camera, but soon wrote off the investment and exited the business.

It has a new social business platform, Quad, having decided that an adjacency into human networking fits its image and competency but social business platform sales are among the most competitive and thankless in the software domain.

Cisco is still a great—albeit struggling—company, but in the end it has no convincing narrative that inspires, embraces or engages existing or new customers with a vision of a new future and a different Cisco.

Successful cognitive reframing results in a convincing narrative that also helps peers to reframe and to see the world differently. It is integral to a mission to offer concrete new experiences for customers, experiences that reshape some small element of their lives through new products and services. The word mission is important. We pointed out earlier that ecosystems thrive on missions.

The difficultly with cognitive reframing lies not in seeing these opportunities, but in convincing tens of thousand of people of their desirability and naturalness, and simultaneously creating the conditions for success. It takes the ability to change many minds.

But that is only one, albeit the most significant, skill of the sapient leader.

We see a number of leadership trends converge in the elastic enterprise, which we will explore in greater detail in the next chapter. But, in addition to cognitive reframing, one other leadership skill is essential.

That skill is the ability to orchestrate.

Leaders lead, of course, but they also inspire, motivate, set goals and strategy, and ultimately form a band of believers that work together for a common purpose.

The type of leadership required in the 21st century is both transformative: capable of reforming the wealth creation system, and entrepreneurial: capable of grasping the new dynamics of resource allocation and organization.

Leaders in the elastic enterprise must be able to orchestrate their peers. They must have the capacity to spur and encourage collaboration and to allow others to lead when appropriate, much as a conductor does when working with an orchestra. Orchestration is critical when working with business ecosystems. The leader must inspire, attract and assure all participants in the business ecosystem that they will benefit from membership.

Orchestration also involves creating the rules and systems that provide the common boundaries in which many different employees and partners can create, contribute, collaborate and be successful.

Creating the conditions for success is a tricky business and requires the use of technology, an understanding of communities, and providing the right tools and data for a diverse community of individuals to get their job done.

Most importantly, orchestration involves values. The only way a leader can relate to peers across many cultures is to embody values that attract approval.

The sapient leader knows that a strong commitment to values can motivate and provide direction.

Steve Jobs' strong, some would say fanatical, commitment to the values of great design, guides Apple's employees.

The power of specific, articulated values gives life and humanness to a corporation. And the values enable those who believe in them to bond and become passionate about the vision, mission, products and services of the company.

The new leadership approaches found in elastic enterprises are not really about personalities, though they may seem that way. While personality traits abound and human frailties exist in elastic enterprise leaders, the elastic enterprise leader thinks, strategizes, and executes differently.

That is why we consider leadership an especially important dynamic of the elastic enterprise.

Simply having the four other dynamics in place does not make an enterprise elastic. A special type of leadership is required.

Put another way, owning a Ferrari will not make you win a race. You need a passionate, skillful and inspired driver who knows what he or she is doing. The first four dynamics give you the Ferrari. With sapient leadership, you win the race.

The ability to work in transformative ways requires, as we said earlier, an ability to reframe situations cognitively.

Cognitive reframing presupposes the intelligence and curiosity to learn about adjacent markets and cultures and to bring elements of those cultures into the host company, the host culture. The sapient leader, therefore, has to know what is going on outside of the core market.

Sapient leaders not only must envision the future, they must also be experts in convergence, the surprising pathways that lead to a new frame of reference.

They need to know what is happening in the global economy and the restructuring of the global demography because that's where future scaled markets are latent.

They will also need to be familiar with the technology of globalization, the business platforms and the power of scaled interaction, sufficient to design and drive the new business framework.

They will see ecosystems as a new business challenge, not as an amorphous something. Figure 4.1 illustrates the relationship between sapient leaders and the business ecosystem.

FIGURE 4.1 The Virtuous Cycle of Sapient Leadership and Business Ecosystems

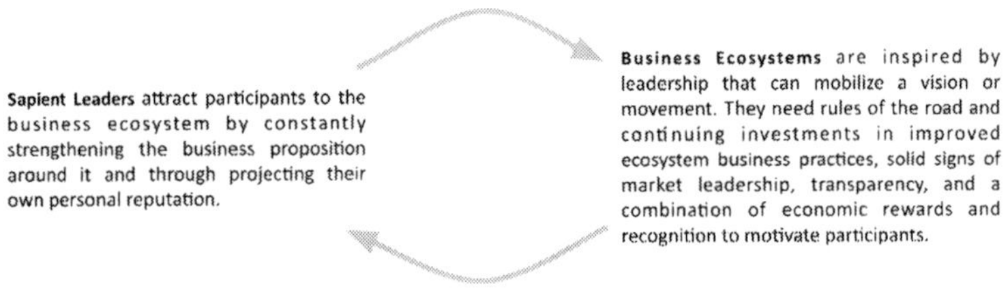

Sapient Leaders attract participants to the business ecosystem by constantly strengthening the business proposition around it and through projecting their own personal reputation.

Business Ecosystems are inspired by leadership that can mobilize a vision or movement. They need rules of the road and continuing investments in improved ecosystem business practices, solid signs of market leadership, transparency, and a combination of economic rewards and recognition to motivate participants.

A viable ecosystem doesn't thrive on a unilateral plan and a push-leadership model. On the contrary, each leader in this new era, whether at Apple, Google, Amazon, Netflix, GE or Caterpillar, leads by a process of design, orchestration, analytics, experimentation and reinvention. The ecosystem is the sandbox for these new process innovation opportunities.

Sapient leaders have an enormous curiosity that pushes them into all these fields and which, in turn, allows them to force their executives to excel in their particular portion of the transforming landscape.

They are capable of playing a pivotal role in the design of a platform, the cultivation of an ecosystem, and the use of data generated through the ecosystem to orchestrate, experiment and adjust their strategy.

But there is also something larger at work among the leaders who are prospering today. Remember those rules and conditions for success we discussed earlier?

Sapient leaders demonstrably learn. They hold open the option for debate even though it may test their "baby." They appear smart because they ensure that their rules are open to question, but at the same time, they take strong positions and vigorously engage in the debate.

They work to win over critics and skeptics. And, if necessary, they will change.

As a consequence, they appear to be tested and wise. Over time, they are increasingly able to formulate innovative and divergent business models where a range of partners—large and small—thrives.

In front of educated, highly intelligent and diverse audiences of ecosystem partners and influencers, they live the right kind of life, in tune with the interests of their partners. They look and sound the part. They embody an attitude, a moral correctness, that can be provocative or irksome or inspiring but can't be called wrong. In short, the sapient leader is authentic.

Building a strategy that puts the future of the enterprise into an apparently unstructured environment, which is what they do, takes intelligence and nerve, but it also takes the trust of all the people around them. It is a big task to take on one person's shoulders but modern leaders are doing just that.

Sapient evokes the sense of intelligence, reflection and nerve that it takes to lead people into a new way of doing things, while maintaining and even building trust across many thousands of loosely coupled relationships.

THE MAIN POINTS REVIEWED

Business ecosystems are complex and highly scaled systems of relationships that are managed through the business platform or multiple business platforms.

These ecosystems are resources for the elastic enterprise but they are resources that, critically, the enterprise must attract and sustain rather than buy.

The need to nurture and sustain the business ecosystem places a new burden on leadership to make an enterprise, its mission and values, attractive to a group of peers. There is no alternative to creating a mission or movement that appeals to peer groups. This is a significant change from all previous leadership requirements.

The leader that proves attractive is a sapient leader, one whose values and skills resonate in a community of peers. But there is more to sapient leadership. Much more.

The idea of the business ecosystem though is much wider than this peer group. Successful enterprises have to develop resource strategies that are highly elastic, and that means engaging with contingent labor forces, crowdsourcing, customer ecosystems and many more elastic resource pools.

In all cases the art of persuasion and influence is becoming the heart of leadership.

To see if you are ready for business ecosystems ask:

1. What aspects of my company portfolio would be best conducted outside of my company if I had a chance of finding exactly the right people?

2. Do we understand how to frame our business process improvements as challenges that anybody outside our field of expertise could understand?

3. Are we comfortable with orchestrating a solution? Or orchestrating a group of followers?

4. How open are we, that is, how comfortable are we with altering our strategies or timetables based on input from outsiders?

5. What experience do we have with managing multiple partnerships? Across networks?

6. Do we have a feel for a "rules of the road"?

7. Which of our technologies or services could we disrupt?

8. What is our reputation as a partner? Do others see us as a desirable partner?

9. How close are we to our existing customers? Do we have customers that we consider partners or co-creators of products, services or strategies?

10. Do our customers innovate for us? With us? Do we know the structure of our customer ecosystems?

11. What is on the periphery of your customer markets?

12. Can we efficiently engage with customers outside of our traditional segments?

13. Are we interested in micro-markets? How do we uncover, understand and engage with the micro-markets in our customer base?

---

[1] Alfred Chandler, The Visible Hand. Belknap Press, 1977

[2] The original crowdsourcing article by Jeff Howe, "The Rise of Crowdsourcing," (http://www.wired.com/wired/archive/14.06/crowds.html) appeared in *Wired* in June 2006, but the best places to keep track of developments are crowdsourcing. org and dailycrowdsource.com.

[3] "Mobile Work: A Way to Make Money by Texting," The Economist, May 2010. See also the work of U.S. start up TxtEagle.

[4] Eric Von Hippel, Jeroen De Jong, Steven Flowers, "Comparing Business and Household Sector Innovation in Consumer Products: Findings from a Representative Study in the UK," SSRN, February 2010.

[5] The Linux open source ecosystem is an exception to the open source culture with 75% of its participants now on salary.

[6] Indeed, Apple's ecosystem continuously throws up discord, for example, over SDK limitation and apps distribution. See Ben Wilson, "iPhone AppStore: Users and Developer Complaints," CNET, July 18, 2008 (www.reviews.cnet.com).

[7] Tim Carmody, "Without Jobs as CEO, Who Speaks for the Arts at Apple?" http://www.wired.com, August 29, 2011.

CHAPTER 5
THE SAPIENT LEADER

The Importance of a New Form of Leadership

Business platforms and business ecosystems introduce new business competencies.

In fact they become a significant new core competency in companies that adopt them. They create an ability to scale business relationships at low cost. They create jobs and new forms of work. They enable new individuals to contribute productively in new ways.

Coupled to the rise of Cloud computing they offer unprecedented elasticity, the flexibility and strength to take a company into adjacent markets, and to outpace the competition.

But all these new capabilities call for a new set of leadership skills.

On the technology side, two profound drivers of change are mobile technologies, that now power the growth of Cloud services, and the sheer scale of computing that many modern platforms are capable of supporting (for example Facebook's 850 million members). Both have ramped up the scale of business interaction in ways that are only manageable through elastic tools.

Having a community of many hundreds of millions of members in constant interaction is no longer an unusual scale of activity. But that calls for a different management approach, and a rapprochement with IT!

Mobile telephony companies for example typically deal with device sales in the several hundred millions a year. Compare Dell, for a while the leading vendor of PCs with 30 million units, to Nokia with 500 million. Modern, global business is a big data environment.

Business analytics in this environment deals with transactions of many billions per day. Google, for example, passed 1.5 billion daily impressions on Google+ within three months of its launch.

To appreciate the power of platforms and ecosystems, you have to get used to large numbers. And the implications of such large numbers need grasping by leaders.

On the non-technological side, trends such as the new phase of globalization, one where emerging economies are winning their spurs on the global stage, the rise of a new forms of market segmentation based on data, the new requirement to attract and assemble resources instead of old school raw materials and capital investment, all call for new ways to lead companies. But not just companies. Leadership today is about being credible in front of a huge ecosystem of partners and customers.

We've chosen to call that new form of leadership "sapient," deliberately to imply a degree of wisdom or sagacity.

While we believe new successful leaders are indeed wise, however, we mean a very specific set of behaviors.

In order to lead well in this environment, leaders need to learn a range of new skills and acquire or enhance specific personal attributes that mark them as leaders of a new type of organization.

They have to be deemed worth following by a highly dispersed ecosystem.

That ecosystem has to perceive the leader as wise enough to know the technological and transformational opportunities that are available to the ecosystem and trust the leader to make the right calls in landing those opportunities.

The leader is in effect working on their behalf, and they are in part judge and jury on his or her competence.

The leader depends on the business ecosystem members as a key resource for the company. You can't buy these resources. The business ecosystem, its members and prospective members need to be attracted and nurtured.

These types of skills accompany new leadership behaviors.

There are six distinctive behaviors that we believe typify sapient leadership.

These behaviors exist alongside characteristics that persuade ecosystem members to follow: evidence of a strong technical and/or customer focus, being at ease with radical adjacency, a convincing public performer, cross-disciplinary experience, an ability to inspire a movement, a leader who has his or her hand up for higher values.

Those six are:

1. **Invention**—All of the sapient leaders we studied are inventors. They generate ideas and ways to grow their business, or, they strongly direct an invention process that is more than just innovation.

2. **Reframing**—Sapient leaders have an ability to reframe and create a new perspective on problems and opportunities. In addition they have the capacity to reframe the vision, mission or values of the enterprise and bring people along with them; they enable everyone in their orbit to reframe.

3. **Attraction and orchestration**—A leader in an elastic enterprise has to attract and orchestrate a huge range of assets outside the firm throughout its business ecosystem.

4. **Influence**—While the tools of the elastic enterprise enable leaders to orchestrate huge ecosystems, they also need to influence, cajole, encourage and incentivize the members of those ecosystems. Influence is an appropriate medium for leading in an open ecosystem full of independent businesses. It can expand without limit whereas other forms of power are limited.

5. **Drawing the lines**—Sapient leaders typically need to define new barriers, for example between influence and

command, or market extension and radical adjacency. They need to draw these lines not just for themselves but also on behalf of an ecosystem. Sapience lies in knowing where to draw the line.

6. **De-risking**—The emerging economy requires a new approach to risk. This economy is global, hyper-competitive and replete with opportunity that leaders are seizing with radical adjacency moves. The sapient leader knows how to prepare for and seize appropriate opportunities and will, as a result, institute very high standards in strategic options portfolio management (see chapter 6).

Steve Jobs: A Quintessential Sapient Leader

Steve Jobs's resignation from his position as CEO of Apple in August of 2011 stunned the worlds of business and the arts, as much as his untimely death saddened people.

By any definition, Steve Jobs left a strong legacy of sapient leadership. He has been called a leader for our times—one who shaped our world.

Perhaps the most formative influence on his leadership approach was his turnaround of Apple after his return to the company in 1996. His successes at Apple, NeXT and Pixar are evidence of *cross-disciplinary* wisdom that also reflects his breadth of experience.

What he brought back to Apple was an enhanced understanding of business, after involving himself in the dynamics of different markets (high performance computing and animation) and their unique requirements. He also brought a broader insight into the range of consumer needs beyond the realms of personal computing.

We mention these characteristics because we see them in other successful leaders at the helm of companies that are on the road to being elastic—the inter-bank communications company SWIFT, Amex, MasterCard, and Thomson Reuters. Here too you will see interdisciplinary backgrounds at the top.

A range of new interests and disciplines is typical of sapient leaders and also illustrates the willingness of sapient leaders to re-*invent* themselves and their companies. These are the characteristics we want to illustrate with the concept of "reframing." Jobs *typically reframed himself* and his company.

One of Jobs' first triumphs was to take the company out of personal computing and into the MP3 market, followed quickly by allying himself to the world of music through iTunes. This remains one of the first and most remarkable *radical adjacency* moves, though more was to come.

The kind of lessons Jobs' career carries are evident in other sapient leaders—Jobs began as a *cross-disciplinary* leader inspired by typography. He went on to *reframe computing* to include the creative arts, and to foster an environment of *invention* in software development, advertising and among users of Apple products.

If we look closer at Job's leadership style we begin to understand the positive dynamic between a sapient leader and an elastic enterprise.

Within the core Apple organization, Jobs operated much like any other CEO.[1] He focused on his top 100 leaders. Those leaders were not all vice presidents, however. Instead, they were the top 100 contributors. In an article in *Fortune* in March of 2008, in his most extensive public interview, Jobs describes his approach:

> We've got 25,000 people at Apple. About 10,000 of them are in the stores. And my job is to work with sort of the top 100 people, that's what I do. That doesn't mean they're all vice presidents. Some of them are just key individual contributors. So when a good idea comes, you know, part of my job is to move it around, just see what different people think, get people talking about it, argue with people about it, get ideas moving among that group of 100

people, get different people together to explore different aspects of it quietly, and, you know—just explore things.[2]

He focused on ideas and avenues for invention and innovation. He also believed in discussion and debate.

Each Monday he ran a meeting inside the company that examined all aspects of the business. He questioned, discussed, debated and held people accountable.[3]

When preparing for his own legendary product presentation events, he actively solicited input, criticism and a rigorous rehearsal schedule to make his presentation "perfect." He held himself to the same standards as everyone else. While this may seem democratic or consensus-based, it is not.

Within Apple, Steve Jobs was an *orchestrator*, but he also commanded and controlled. He was comfortable with both styles. In his comments on the development of the iPhone, Jobs noted the following about his role:

> It was a great challenge. Let's make a great phone that we fall in love with. And we've got the technology. We've got the miniaturization from the iPod. We've got the sophisticated operating system from Mac. Nobody had ever thought about putting operating systems as sophisticated as OS X inside a phone, so that was a real question. We had a big debate inside the company whether we could do that or not. And that was one where I had to adjudicate it and just say, 'We're going to do it. Let's try.' The smartest software guys were saying they can do it, so let's give them a shot. And they did.[4]

He encouraged debate and in the process he and his team reframed the concept of the phone and the mission of the firm.

What is not so widely known about Apple's iPhone and iPad is the extent of *de-risking* that went on before the product launch.

The iPad was in fact ready in prototype prior to the iPhone[5], but probably drawing on his experience with the failed Newton (the first Apple tablet device, produced in the 1990s), Jobs held off launching the iPad until the iPhone was a sure success.

Inside the company he managed with a combination of invention, influence, orchestration, debate, command, collaborative development and intelligent de-risking.

He used the same behaviors outside of Apple. He did not, and indeed could not, use edicts to command or control the various players in the Apple business ecosystem.

Think of those thousands of apps developers, the legions of musicians, filmmakers and now writers who make up the production end of the business ecosystem. And the retailers that sell Apple products. And the independent authors who comment on the company; the analysts whose views are reflected in the share price.

These were not there for anyone to command. Rather, he influenced them. And he did this through a huge investment in several aspects of the Apple business.

A flawless business platform de-risked the launch of iTunes and iPhone: First Jobs ensured his engineers created a near flawless business platform to support iTunes and then the App Store. Dating back to the release of the iTunes project in early 2003, the business platform has evolved in scale and in complexity.

Apple launched it first in the U.S. and then gradually across other countries.

In contrast, in 2009, mobile phone competitor Nokia released its apps and content store, Ovi, in 35 countries simultaneously, prioritizing global coverage over usability. It flopped and the subsequent ecosystem fallout played a large part in Nokia's decline.

Business Ecosystem development: Apple was able to attract an exceptionally large ecosystem of apps developers to its iPhone products, based in part on bringing its existing developer community into the new vision.

The scale of that ecosystem quickly rose to more than 300,000.

The figure is not wholly exceptional—many companies have a developer ecosystem running into six or seven figures, for example the SAP community network has 2.4 million members.

Apple was proposing that developers come join them in a new journey, and create lightweight apps for a product that would never sell in the numbers that competitors like Nokia were selling. The surge to join the developer ecosystem remains an amazing case study of *attraction, assembly and orchestration.*

Investment in influence: The very high quality of Apple event marketing and advertising also works as a key differentiator. There is no drop in quality from the beauty of the company's devices to the projection of its public image.

At the same time it was able to influence that new body of opinion represented by social media, bloggers, independent web sites and conventional media and convince them that its new plans were gold.

When Google and partner HTC launched the first Android smartphone, the G1, in 2008, Apple's iPhone outnumbered it in social media references by 12:1. At that time there was no Apple launch news of any kind.

Jobs mastered the ecosystem of *influence.* It took Brin and Page a lot longer to learn.

The amplification of his leadership influence across an ecosystem, one that he could not actually own, is the true measure of how this new approach to leadership was received in the marketplace.

Our premise is that the elastic enterprise is creating a need for new leadership competencies like this and in turn sapient leaders are inventing new capabilities for the enterprise.

We believe this reciprocal relationship between the elastic enterprise and leadership is historically unique.

Sapient leadership is in its earliest stage and will develop and mature over the coming decades. Just as General Electric, Ford and General Motors forged new leadership traits for the industrial enterprise, pioneers like Amazon, Apple and lesser known lights like USAA will evolve the new traits of sapient leadership.

The Six Behaviors of the Sapient Leader

Let's look at the key behaviors of the sapient leader in more detail, bearing in mind that these behaviors are conditioned by exceptional economic conditions and the need to adopt and learn new behaviors.

Invention

Thomas Edison, one of the most famous inventors in history, also started many companies, including long-term successes Con Edison, the first electric utility, and the mega-corporation General Electric. Posthumously, Steve Jobs has been dubbed "the Edison" of our generation.

We think invention is an essential behavior for any leader who wants to run a successful elastic enterprise, simply because of the times we live in. The drive to create something new akin to the founder mentality, drives invention even in stable times.

Sapient leaders hold invention near and dear. They are typically founders. There is a trait among them that is very close to the founder mentality. Some, like Jobs, are literally founders, but even those that work within somebody else's organization have an ability to re-invent it and to inject the founder dynamic.

Francisco González, who leads BBVA, the Hispanic bank, is a case in point.

He took over the bank just prior to BBVA's privatization and reshaped it into one of the most successful integrated banks globally. González previously owned a brokerage firm that he founded.

Kenneth Chenault, who has catapulted Amex back to significance in financial services, earned his leadership position by reinventing Travel Related Services (TRS), the dominant revenue division within Amex.

Kevin Hartz, founder of Eventbrite, insists that his company is part of a new wave of businesses that are enabling people to create new economic activity. This is a point reiterated by many young leaders—they are not just innovating a new service, they are inventing part of the new economy.

Sapient leaders, in other words, go beyond innovation.

Of course, many sapient leaders are actual founders—Steve Jobs, Marc Benioff at Salesforce.com, Pony Ma at Tencent in China, Jon von Tetzchner, formerly at European browser company Opera.

Mike Perlis, the CEO who is busy reinventing Forbes Media as an elastic enterprise, previously founded New England Publications and was also responsible for reinventing Ziff David around Internet content and issues.

The best sapient leaders project an enthusiasm for invention that is contagious. It spreads within their companies and across their business ecosystems.

As A.G. Lafley illustrated in his turnaround of P&G, the superior power of P&G's distribution system offered little prospects for growth without an equivalent engine for invention. Once he refurbished P&G's invention engine, P&G began to thrive and grow again.

An elastic enterprise needs leaders that understand and love invention.

The business platform that underpins the elastic enterprise is typically an invention engine.

It supports and scales a business ecosystem that typically generates a large number of ideas and creativity.

But the platform itself is a continuously evolving invention: look for examples at the fast-evolving area of mobile document access, Microsoft's SkyDrive and Apple's iCloud.

Both Microsoft and Apple are in the process of inventing how to combine Cloud, mobile and productivity apps.

Invention is at the platform level, usage, and interfaces. It renders a simple service, yet represents a complex invention process.

Another feature of sapient leaders is that they are typically good at reinventing themselves. Chenault began his adult life as a historian (as did George Halvorson at Kaiser Permanente). Thomas Glocer at Thomson Reuters worked in a global legal practice before joining Reuters. González was an economist and then a stockbroker.

Fred Smith, founder and inventor of FedEx (originally called Federal Express), began in 1973 with a fleet of aircraft to transport packages. But success required a series of inventions in order to establish and maintain leadership and growth, beginning with the hub and spokes distribution model, the COSMOS centralized computer logistics system (1979), the FedEx SuperTracker handheld barcode package data entry system (1986), the PowerShip online/real-time package tracking system (1988) and the Internet-based customer information system (1994).

The inventions grew into an integrated logistics business platform that became a separate division and ultimately led to a business ecosystem of partners that handled traditional and specialized inventory and distribution requirements for global corporations.[6] Today FedEx is a multi-model transportation and logistics company.

Reframing

In 1985, David Bowie authorized his entire musical catalog to be converted to digital audio CDs.

At the time, neither he nor the music recording industry understood that this was a harbinger of transformation.

With the Internet and increasingly powerful personal computers, music fans began to convert digital audio CDs into digital MP3 files. Soon massive libraries of digital music were being copied and shared by millions of fans globally. By the year 2000, creative property rights were in turmoil and the music recording industry was on a long road of decline.

Steve Jobs viewed this as an opportunity. The trick was to figure out a way to compensate creative talent and record labels while unleashing the pent-up demand in the marketplace for a different type of music consumption.

Jobs' talent was to help the music industry reframe its business around the sale of single tracks, a defining characteristic of music file sharing but something the industry didn't want to do—it made its millions through album sales.

The risk Jobs took was to invest in a platform the likes of which hadn't yet been seen. This was a platform that enabled lawful, paid, music downloads. And it had to work on an unprecedented scale—thousands of musicians, potentially billions of downloads, all properly transacted and accounted for.

The communities of musicians who make music were a ready-made but skeptical ecosystem. The platform would have to deliver flawlessly for them.

It would need content visibility tools, customer engagement tools (like, eventually, Genius, the lightweight MP3s that Apple went onto produce) and a commerce engine that would do all the accounting in a trustworthy manner.

This was a high order of invention made to look ordinary by how well it worked. And through it Steve Jobs helped reframe music as it faced decimation by illegal file sharing and downloads.

Many leaders have an uncanny ability to unlock potential. Sapient leaders, however, are able to draw together these new elements—the platform, the ecosystem, the connectors and increasingly as we go into the future, the Cloud, to invent new ways of unlocking value and serving customers.

There are critical cognitive skills that underlie the ability to reframe a situation in this way—or in any positive way. Research by Dr. Stellan Ohlsson at the University of Chicago indicates that people typically avoid reframing. They try to apply old solutions to new situations. To gain a new insight requires that we stop doing that. David Rock, in *Your Brain at Work*, summarizes this research:

> Ohlsson's research shows that people have to stop themselves from thinking along one path before they can find a new idea. 'The projection of prior experience has to be actively suppressed and inhibited,' Ohlsson explains. This is surprising, as we tend to think that inhibition is a bad thing, that it will lower your creativity. But as long as your prior approach is most dominant, has the highest level of activation, you will get more refined variations of the same approach, but nothing genuinely new comes to the fore.[7]

So when sapient leaders reframe a situation, they are in a sense enabling themselves and encouraging others to abandon old, familiar approaches to solving a problem and look at the situation in a new way.

Interestingly, our brains need to explicitly inhibit the old way of thinking in order to properly and productively explore a new approach.

Sapient leaders essentially initiate a huge interrupt in the way everyone is thinking. In a sense they are rebooting the public perspective.

Neurobiological research indicates that this approach is more than simply a "mind game" or mental gymnastics.

Reframing is the cognitive process of taking an assessment of a situation and determining whether new conditions merit a rethinking of accepted limits. In a rapidly changing world, the probabilities are in favor of rethinking and reframing.

Attraction and orchestration

Attraction and orchestration are among the most important skills in the new leadership armory.

Attracting and orchestrating an ecosystem is as vital as having working capital. It is the modern equivalent.

It is particularly important to attract and orchestrate resources for a new service or product—but that is a daunting task.

Mobile phone giant Nokia had device sales of around 435 million units per year by 2008[8] Yet Nokia allowed Apple to outpace it in the development and deployment of apps, even though Nokia had an existing ecosystem of developers.

Again Ovi is instructive.

When Ovi launched some months after the App Store it noticeably lacked a significant apps' catalogue. Ovi at one stage boasted it had reached a million downloads a month at a time when Apple had already passed 1 billion in total downloads.

From launch onwards the platform had technical difficulties. So even though Nokia in some sense "owned" the mobile device market and had huge financial muscle, it failed to convince apps developers to jump on board in sufficient numbers to prevent its embarrassment by Apple.

Take, also, a company like Amazon.

Amazon has thousands of writers submitting and marketing books through its new e-reader platform, Kindle. The Kindle Direct Publishing tool very quickly accumulated 700,000 titles. Like Apple's App Store it grew scale astonishingly fast.

In addition it has a growing community of apps developers for its new tablet—the Kindle Fire.

In another part of its business it has a community of reviewers, the general reviewer community and its closer, more trusted Vine[9] community of reviewers.

Elsewhere it has a community of customers around its Cloud services. And of course it has thousands of employees.

In contrast to Nokia, Amazon has kept a pretty good scorecard with its communities.

It hired reviewers when it first set up its recommendation system. That meant it could seed its retail site with reviewer content.

Prior to launching Fire it opened its own Android apps market, so that by the time Fire launched there was already a healthy population of apps that would populate the new Amazon tablet.

Apple and Amazon have been very effective at attracting independently owned, creative resources.

Attracting participants in an ecosystem requires vision and leadership.

Jobs was at his best when promising to change the world. Vision was never an issue. Bezos is not so high flown in rhetoric but his record of invention is now so strong that he has no problem convincing developers and content providers that they will profit by investing their time with him.

Business ecosystems also need very clear contractual documentation—they are characterized by democratic principles in this regard. Old models of business ecosystems, like Nokia's apps prior to Ovi, were characterized by special deals with large content providers.

Apple's contracts are characterized by simple universal deals where each developer receives a standard percentage of the sales price of their app.

The three key elements of successful attraction skills are:

- Vision.
- Uniform terms and conditions and a sense that this is for everyone without favor.
- Faultless technical execution to win peer respect.

If those elements give you a chance to attract resources, you also need to know how to keep an ecosystem in good shape.

Keeping an ecosystem healthy requires great orchestration skills.

In an orchestra, the conductor uses the musical score and his or her own skill and artistic sensibility to coordinate the individual performance of each musician. This is a special meeting of peers with musicians often of the highest caliber under the conductor's direction.

To orchestrate means to arrange a collection of elements to produce a desired effect.

In an elastic enterprise, the business platform and business ecosystem are part of the musical score along with the business strategy. The sapient leader brings the elements together and influences them by respecting the peer status of participants, and by amplifying the ecosystem's external leadership

Influence

Sapient leadership is first and foremost about the ability to capture the minds and hearts of an entire business ecosystem; a diverse group of people whom they do not employ and whom they need if their strategy is to function. They must win them over and influence their aspirations and behavior.

For the leader, the ecosystem represents a new set of assets. Influence is the essential communications tool in a new corporate structure that is, in effect, a pluralistic community of peers, marked by cultural diversity, serving a multiplicity of customer preferences.

To be a leader is to influence these others.

While command and control, the staples of the industrial enterprise leader, will not go away, they are less effective and can be dysfunctional in the elastic enterprise.

Warren Bennis is credited with being one of the first scholars to argue for a more democratic and influence-based model of leadership in environments marked by change and complexity. Bennis also advanced the notion of the follower as an important participant.

The late Peter Drucker noted that as complex organizations move into the twenty-first century, leaders must operate more as conductors of an orchestra and view their employees and followers more as volunteers, rather than as subordinates or indentured servants.

Economists too have noted the power of influence.

When Stephen Klepper, professor at Carnegie Mellon and recipient of the 2011 Global Award for Entrepreneurship Research, examined the evolution of large companies in the U.S., he observed that a decisive factor in their ability to survive and prosper was the ability of the leader to influence the company in the face of complex ownership structures.[10]

Klepper has found that companies with diffuse ownership structures prove to be less effective at making radical decisions. Diffuse ownership limits their ability to change. Executives leading enterprises with diffuse ownership are more dependent on keeping the markets happy and are often unable to muster the followers needed to be decisive and change strategic direction.

Conversely, companies with a tightly knit ownership structure are often able to make radical decisions. BMW, the German auto company, for example, is a listed entity but is owned to a significant degree by the Quandt family

The Quandts have been able to hire and empower strong leaders at different levels of the organization. They empower them with the slogan "lead, don't follow."

Seeking out leadership opportunities is what makes BMW tick.

BMW reinvented competitive advantage in the car industry in the 2000s through emphasizing shape and emotion over engineering quality—yet retained a reputation as one of the best-engineered cars.

Lately they have opted for a post-ownership strategy for autos and are seeking ways to move beyond the car itself as their main offer to customers. It's a radical move made possible by strong ownership.

As influence becomes more important, CEOs become more effective when they can influence diffuse groups of owners. Not an easy task. But an emphasis on influence can change the dynamics of a company.

The sapient leader must thrive in a world of rapid change and highly scaled partnerships and sometimes diffuse ownership. Leaders of elastic enterprises must be able to build influence among many constituencies. Command and control approaches in this environment become an anemic and illusory source of power.

One essential ingredient in influence is access to an information infrastructure that encompasses the ecosystem—independent web sites, fans, media, bloggers and analysts—that see eye to eye with the leader. In fact it pays to seed such an infrastructure (see our discussion earlier of the HTC G1 launch).

There is one more reason for an emphasis on influence as a source of leadership power.

Elastic enterprise leadership requires a team of leaders.

In other words, leadership must be distributed across the organization. The elastic enterprise also depends on sapient leaders to lead a diverse community of partners across a geographically distributed business ecosystem. Since no single leader can be omnipresent, the success of the elastic enterprise depends on virtually everyone exercising some type of leadership role, somewhere, in some way, through influence.

Drawing the lines

Sapient leaders also command their organizations when necessary.

Sapient leaders often have to work with partners in their business ecosystem that operate "command-heavy" business cultures.

Steve Jobs was legendary for his intolerance of failure and his almost dictatorial approach on design decisions.

Jobs also had to work with Foxconn, a command-heavy and controversial contract manufacturer of the iPhone and iPad. Apple could not have met the demand for their products without the precision manufacturing capabilities at Foxconn. Time will tell whether Foxconn can soften their command-heavy practices.

Similarly, Jeff Bezos is known for strong command-oriented decision making. His weekly four-hour management meetings are legendary—more akin to a thesis defense—with colleagues expected to have quantitative answers rather than qualitative opinions.[11]

Early in Amazon's history, Bezos was known for his intolerance for ho-hum ideas and his unrelenting drive for innovation. More recently, Bezos has demonstrated his penchant for root-cause analysis and Kaizen continuous improvement discipline in operations.

Bezos also chooses to deal with Foxconn's command-heavy manufacturing culture since they manufacture the Kindle. He also deals with other command-heavy cultures that support their elastic compute Cloud division.

But what defines the sapient brand of command is the way that the sapient leader effectively blends command behavior with influence and orchestration behaviors.

Sapient leaders have an instinct for where to draw the line between the two—it is part of their persona, and they get it wrong as well as right.

Participants in a business ecosystem will tolerate failures though if they see the leader wrestling constructively with those dilemmas. They are intolerant of dictatorial behavior that covers up a lack of intuition or wisdom. As Reed Hastings of Netflix has found, when the markets tore into his share price (wiping 50% off it in 10 weeks, July 13, 2011 to September 19, 2011) after he made a miscued call on strategy, colleagues and ecosystem members have not deserted him. Peer respect seems to be a persistent factor in the share price's recovery.

A recent article in *The Economist* points out that Steve Jobs was roundly criticized early in his career for being a control freak:

"Mr. Jobs had a reputation as a control freak, and his critics complained that the products and systems he designed were closed and inflexible, in the name of greater ease of use.[12]"

Ironically, that "freakishness" and command orientation about design also enhanced his influence and ability to orchestrate vast numbers of followers in the Apple business ecosystem.

Bezos, too, has a host of critics. For many years, critics labeled him a buffoon and castigated Amazon for its lack of profits. However, Bezos was not swayed and in fact largely ignored the criticism, insisting that investors must wait. Eventually, Amazon became wildly profitable and Bezos now has his fan club, including such notables at Warren Buffett.

Sapient leaders also exercise command behavior in business ecosystems.

It is easy to characterize business ecosystems as a free-for-all or an unstructured agglomeration of human activity, but that is an oversimplification. Business ecosystems must also have order and structure and, to some degree, control.

For this reason, sapient leaders embed command and control mechanisms into the business platforms that support the business ecosystem and at times publicly challenge the policies or practices of partners in those business ecosystems.

Typically a business ecosystem functions around standardized terms and conditions. The terms can apply to partner companies like developers, individual creatives like writers, or customers. Business ecosystems thrive on standardized terms, contracts and procedures (often embedded in business platform software) to legitimate essential command and control mechanisms.

Command and control mechanisms allow many people to join the ecosystem but they also impose expectations and obligations. Often terms and conditions include a clause that allows the core company to change the terms and conditions without notice. These uniform terms are accepted because they are uniform—there is no favoritism. The ground rules apply to everyone.

Sapient leaders must sometimes make a decision or policy change that will upset some of the members of the business ecosystem.

Maintaining awareness in the ecosystem that those calls will be made, and made for the right reasons, is part of the command obligation for the sapient leader.

Apple made those kinds of calls around the Adobe Flash Player.

It consistently refused to allow Flash apps on its devices. The move is important because there are tens of thousands of creative content-related items that could find their way into the App Store that are written for Flash. By not accepting those, Steve Jobs disappointed a huge and potentially lucrative developer community.

The argument around Flash for Apple reached a peak in the spring of 2010. Adobe responded by calling Apple's act a slap in the face for developers. Yet even with the weight of Adobe on the protagonist side, this is an argument that Apple and Steve Jobs won. Adobe withdrew Flash mobile in November 2011.

Sapient leaders know how and when to play their hand, when to invent, reframe, influence, orchestrate and when to command. The key is uniformity: treating everyone alike; treating the small guy like the big guy. That alone is a difficult change for many corporations.

De-risking

As we noted earlier, sapient leaders have a strong commitment to invention and for many it is their strongest trait. But it amounts to little without bringing invention to market. The latter requires a very strong dose of discipline, determination, will, doggedness, rigor and patience.

In markets where radical adjacency moves are becoming the norm, companies are placing big bets on the future. And the future might lie in a different market with a different product or service— take a look at HP's recent $10 billion purchase of the specialist search company Autonomy.

To de-risk radical adjacency, leaders need the sweat part to function well. They can't afford to carry laggards. De-risking relies on a determined effort to perfect a course of action, whether an invention or strategy, and not let it see the light of day until success looks most likely. But while sweat is only one part of de-risking, it's an important part.

An elastic enterprise faces many potential courses of action and de-risking at that point becomes less about the process and more about how to deal with new economic circumstances. Elastic enterprises have shown themselves to be capable of moving swiftly into new markets and driving radical adjacencies—Google, for example, into mobile and into productivity apps.

Each adjacency is filled with risk. But the risk is also a reflection of a new optionality. A sapient approach to this risk is to develop a *strategic options portfolio* (more of which in Chapter 6).

A strategic options portfolio is a register of well-worked-out options, primed and ready to go. Apple had the iPad in the pipeline years before it launched. Jobs wanted to see the iPhone succeed first. The iPad stayed in the strategic options portfolio.

Google has a large strategic options portfolio through its acquisitions and venture capital fund.

BMW is developing one through its $100 million "personal mobility" fund.

GE develops strategic options through its Ecomagination and Healthymagination initiatives.

The point of these moves is they create options and options allow leaders to de-risk implementation.

In the era of adjacency it is important to have intelligence about adjacent areas of business, and to be cognizant of opportunity where markets are converging or taste is changing. Jobs took his opportunity in the music industry, an area quite alien to Apple at the time (and then in mobile). But his strategic options portfolio, through acquisition and in-house development was rich enough for him to pick his moment (see Figures 3.4 and 3.5).

THE MAIN POINTS REVIEWED:

Sapient leaders need to master two classes of skills.

The first is the technology that goes into the new business platform, and the continuous data that scaled interaction creates. The second is to build credibility and to interact with a large peer group of independent business people.

They need to have a cross-cultural, cross-disciplinary background, one that allows them to communicate with a diverse peer community.

They will also have a founder's mentality and be conversant with invention. They will seek out advantage the way founders do but they will also have the wisdom to manage strategy in a new way, developing rich strategic options portfolios, leaning on their platform and ecosystem data to signal the right time to execute on radically adjacent market moves.

To see if you qualify as a sapient leader ask:

1. Have I ever acted as a founder and where might I get founder experience?
2. Did I ever invent anything? Where can I get this experience?
3. Do I like to reframe? Do I find emotional resonance and fulfillment in the process of reframing?
4. Does reframing give me and others motivation and new sense of meaning and purpose?
5. Are there experiences outside my main work flow or functional competency that were formative in how I act?
6. What different cultures do I connect with? Can I create a deal that they would find appealing from their background and point of view?
7. Do I present well in front of my peers?
8. Am I comfortable with influence and persuasion?

9. Can I orchestrate? Do I thrive on it?

10. Am I respected rather than feared?

11. Do I act as a leader among equals?

12. What movement do I want to lead? Do I see latent or potential movements in my company looking for a leader? Could they drive invention, a reframe, or transformation?

13. Does the concept of a movement make sense in the context of my leadership style?

14. What vision am I trying to realize?

15. Does the vision create passion in others?

16. Can I project it to those who are not my employees? Can that vision captivate a business ecosystem?

---

[1] Many accounts have surfaced about Steve Jobs and his idiosyncrasies and have been fully chronicled in Walter Isaacson's celebrated biography, Steve Jobs, Simon and Schuster, New York, 2011. Our purpose here is to focus on what we believe are the key features of sapient leadership and why they are necessary for an elastic enterprise.

[2] Betsy Morris, "Steve Jobs Speaks Out," Fortune, March 7, 2008.

[3] Carmine Gallo, The Presentation Secrets of Steve Jobs: How to be Insanely Great in Front of Any Audience. New York: McGraw-Hill, 2010.

[4] Ibid.

[5] John Paczkowski, "D8 Video: Steve Jobs on the Origins of the iPad," June 1, 2010, http://allthingsd.com/20100601/d8-video-steve-jobs-on-the-origins-of-the-ipad/

[6] For an inside look at FedEx and its leadership and management practices, see James C. Wetherbe, The World on Time: The 11 Management Principles That Made FedEx an Overnight Sensation, Knowledge Exchange, 1996.

[7] David Rock, Your Brain at Work: Strategies for Overcoming Distraction, Regaining Focus, and Working Smarter All Day Long, New York: HarperCollins, 2009.

[8] Marguerite Reardon, "Cell Phone Sales Hit 1 Billion Mark," CNET, February 27,2008, http://news.cnet.com/8301-10784_3-9881022-7.html

[9] http://www.amazon.com/gp/vine.

[10] Haydn Shaughnessy, "Large Firms and the Growth of Start-up Culture: A Key Dependency in the Age of Innovation," *Innovation Management*, March 14, 2011.

[11] Fred Vogelstein, "Mighty Amazon Jeff Bezos has been hailed as a visionary and put down as a goofball. He's proved critics wrong by forging a winning management strategy built on brains, guts, and above all, numbers," *Fortune*, May 26, 2003, http://money.cnn.com/magazine/fortune/fortune_archive/2003/05/26/343082/index.htm.

[12] "The Magician: The Revolution that Steve Jobs Led is only Just the Beginning." *The Economist*, October 8, 2011. www.economist.com/node/21531529.

CHAPTER 6
STRATEGY TRANSFORMED

Elastic enterprises are admired for many reasons. But, ultimately, how they compete generates the greatest attention.

One remarkable characteristic is the way elastic enterprises introduce new products or services and invade new industries and market segments where they have little or no prior expertise.

In short, elastic enterprises compete differently.

They do that in part because they have access to the five dynamic elements we have described above. But those dynamics also yield the information flow and capabilities to build extensive strategic options portfolios.

Elastic enterprises provide their leaders, employees, partners and investors with a superior portfolio of strategic options for success, growth and wealth creation.

The Concept of Continuous Active Strategy

Elastic enterprises use what we call a *continuous active strategy*.

Continuous active strategy is a process where the enterprise continuously monitors, revises and revitalizes strategic plans. It is a conceptual innovation in its own right and requires new data processing tools as well as a new management philosophy.

Done right it provides a systematic approach to anticipating and adapting rapidly to changing market conditions. But more importantly it allows an enterprise to impose its will on new markets.

In an instantaneously connected world with substantial mass differentiation, a firm must cycle its business strategy quickly, deliver broader product and service innovations to a wider variety of markets, and execute with minimal risk. And it also needs to lead, to create new markets, and new niches.

To do this, business strategy must be kept fresh. Execution has to take place against a backdrop of an array of strategic options that leaders can deploy as they understand new market developments or when market demand appears to be maturing.

Those strategic options are increasingly a matter of daily bread to leaders in elastic enterprises. They don't wait until they see change before they look to new opportunities. They create the opportunity portfolio actively.

Companies like Apple, and indeed we know this of P&G too, check their numbers every day. They manage vast portfolios of opportunity from a dashboard. They also use it to galvanize a rather large and diverse leadership team. The nature of an instantaneously connected world is that opportunity and risk can break out anywhere, anytime.

When the tsunami struck in Japan, Apple's touch-screen supplies were threatened. The tragic floods in Thailand in the fall of 2011 significantly reduced disk-drive supplies. As the economic crisis hit Greece, many major companies had to quickly uncover suppliers with healthier credit ratings and more stable regimes.

Unexpected demand for Apple's iPhone 4s required a closely monitored global product rollout strategy throughout the fall of 2011 and into 2012.

Apple's CEO Tim Cook commented during their FY 2012 First Quarter Results Conference call on January 24, 2012, that continued strategic review would be necessary as they managed outsized demand for the iPhone 4s in China.

The elastic enterprise has to master the information flows and other big data generated by business platforms and business ecosystems that let them identify newer, better, cheaper sources of supply, or better, more inventive labor. They need to be able to turn the right switch when risk factors get to be intolerable or when opportunity arises.

As seen in Figure 6-1, the business platform and business ecosystem generate new types of data and insights for the enterprise. Leadership today needs to view that information in terms of a continuous active strategy process.

FIGURE 6.1 The Context for Continuous Active Strategy in the Elastic Enterprise

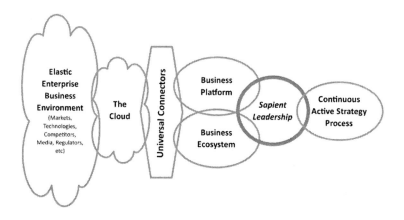

Continuous active strategy takes place at all these levels of granularity, from meta-strategy, to the day-to-day running of a globally distributed business.

There is now an even more granular basis to strategy than ever before. It's one of the difficulties many leaders cannot surmount. They and their teams need to be highly proactive on data, trends and options.

A Closer Look at Continuous Active Strategy

How can we best characterize that highly complex world?

With a continuous active strategy, sapient leaders change course, if need be, or add to their strategy, in weeks not years. They use big data to fact-check their strategy in real time—especially during experiments or the launch of a new venture.

They work with a robust set of strategic options that might have been generated by their data pool or by employees or by their business ecosystems and customers.

And they perfect their game, orchestrating a repertoire of planned and possible plays with a constant eye on the changing conditions of the new global marketplace.

We've found that new element must be added to the strategy process. Figure 6.2 shows four key constructs that support and structure the continuous active strategy process as we observed elastic enterprises in action.

Figure 6.2 Elements of a Continuous Active Strategy Process

Executives must have structures to guide and anchor a more frequent and dynamic strategic decision making process:

1. **Meta-strategy**—sapient leadership, vision, values, aspirations, strategic intents, policies, CAPX, R&D, mega-trends. The meta-strategy provides the long-term view and also provides the structure where the long-term vision and the big moves can be explored, debated, refined and set.

2. **The active strategy playbook**—experimental plays; current plays; and contingent plays, timelines, schedules. The active strategy playbook is the bridge between the long-term moves and tactical execution. Note that since many new options are being generated by business ecosystem partners, detailed understanding of product usage in the field, and R&D, the executive must be able to array these options in terms of potential plays that anticipate market developments. The active strategy playbook is the "work-in-process" domain where strategic options are assessed both in terms of near-term strategic plays and meta-strategic plays. Note that the active strategy playbook is judged according to performance objectives set by the executive team.

3. **The strategic options portfolio**—options, options under consideration, real options. This is the inventory of all the viable and future options available to the executive team. Strategic options include: new products, new product features, product improvements, new inventions, product extensions, business platform extensions, new services and service features, potential acquisitions, deals, new major partners, and so on. Each may be categorized and analyzed based on expected value and timing considerations. As the probability and value of the strategic option grows, it may become part of the active strategy playbook.

4. **Radical adjacency**—acquisitions or organic initiatives that take the enterprise into markets where management and employees have no current experience

Execution

On the execution side, elastic enterprise leaders have unparalleled tools to redirect enterprise activity.

They can add new features to the business platform. They can ask ecosystem partners to add new features to products or services—beyond features that partners add through their own innovative efforts. They can recruit new partners to the business ecosystem.

Apple provides an early example of how a continuous active strategy transforms the strategic process and the enterprise itself.

Within weeks of the iPhone launch in late June 2007, the hacker community had hacked the iPhone, enabling them to capitalize on Apple's innovation, yet no official SDK existed that would allow developers to create products for the iPhone.

From a developer's perspective an iPhone without an official software development kit (SDK) was Dead On Arrival.

Why not allow independent developers to develop applications for the iPhone? Palm had provided an SDK for its Palm device many years earlier and Apple provided an SDK for its Macintosh computers. Why was such an important feature missing in such a hot product as the iPhone?

Apple had no intention of immediately opening the iPhone to the development community. But four months later, in October 2007, Steve Jobs and Apple reversed its position and accelerated the release of the iPhone SDK.

> Let me just say it: We want native third party applications on the iPhone, and we plan to have an SDK in developers' hands in February. We are excited about creating a vibrant third party developer community around the iPhone and enabling hundreds of new applications for our users.[1]

In an uncharacteristic and unprecedented statement, Apple radically accelerated its timetable for the iPhone SDK.

Apple released its first version of its app development environment, and announced the App Store, in February 2008. This was an early example of continuous active strategy where the ecosystem interacted with the enterprise to create an unprecedented product cascade into the market. The ecosystem, in effect, not only accelerated, but also sharpened Apple's strategy.

Meta-Strategy

All enterprises have some type of meta-strategy. An elastic enterprise is no exception and Amazon is a case in point.

At its inception, Jeff Bezos wanted Amazon.com to stand for customer satisfaction and to have a product for every letter in the alphabet.

The meta-strategy was and is big on ambition and it established a long-term road map around which partners and ecosystems can align. Having a meta-strategy of scope keeps analysts and the ecosystem alive to the range of opportunities that a sapient leader like Bezos, with an elastic enterprise, can create.

It reflects the vision, mission and values of the enterprise. It also reflects the dreams, though. It introduces that piece of magic that excites a modern entrepreneur. It encompasses very long-term hunches and what customers will likely desire. Meta strategy, for example, led Amazon to the Kindle and to Cloud services.

Other parts of the meta-strategy reflect more practical matters.

For some companies capital budgeting is critical to ensure that the right level of resources is available for large-ticket items (e.g., data warehouses, business platforms, R&D). Major policies also come under the province of meta-strategy.

This part of strategy, part mission, part dream and part practicality, is updated in the context of *continuous active strategy.*

For example, Apple and Steve Jobs had a meta-strategy around the types of technology customers should have, principally hand-held devices of increasing sophistication but with exceptional ease of use. But as the technology evolved, Apple developed new products, saw its fortunes grow and spotted opportunity in new areas, in part in response to the contributions of its business ecosystem partners.

In the light of these developments the meta-strategy evolved to include advertising and TV.

The Active Strategy Playbook

The active strategy playbook contains the active plays that a company has in motion at any one time alongside the strategic options portfolio, which includes all options to change or reinforce a direction

The playbooks spell out the continuous active strategy, and enable an executive team to integrate its plans, contingencies, hypotheses and alternative courses of action.

Apple's launch of the iPad provides a great example of how meta-strategy and the active strategy playbook work together and drive the continuous active strategy process.

At the time of the iPad launch in 2010, Apple was (at meta-strategy level):

- considering the acquisition of a voice synthesized assistant, Siri (acquired in April 2010, subsequently deployed on the iPhone 4 in October 2011)
- finalizing the acquisitions of Fast Chips and Intrinsity to buttress its hardware expertise
- developing its new Cloud datacenter in North Carolina (rumored late 2009)
- rumored to be moving soon into television in a big way
- expanding iOS and its next-generation iPhone (iPhone 4)
- finalizing the second generation of slimmed down laptops MacBook Air and a more powerful series of the MacBook Pro computers
- filing numerous patents regarding touch, gestures, etc.

And this is just what we know from publicly available information.

Given all of this, what did Apple's active strategy playbook for the iPad in late 2009 and early 2010 look like? We can infer retrospectively the following market-related elements about the iPad:

1. Apple had significant information from its business platform and business ecosystem about how customers were using the iPhone, debates about screen size on the iPhone and requests from customers and developers for more screen "real estate."

2. Apple expected a hardware revision within a year (iPad 2) because this was an entirely new device category and it had already established this pattern with the iPhone. So iPad 1 would offer a significant learning opportunity and test of key product hypotheses related to information consumption, form factor, touch dynamics, software capabilities, immersive experience and PC substitution.

3. A larger form factor than iPhone would appeal to new customers and new partners, further extending the business ecosystem and new markets (e.g., publishing industry, including books, periodicals and newspapers).

4. Having a larger battery and longer battery life than iPhone means it can be an effective information consumption and entertainment appliance.

5. Synergies and common iOS (the operating system) with iPhone radically reduce learning time for a new technology device for customers, developers and for the entire Apple business ecosystem.

6. The ability to use thousands of familiar iPhone apps from the App Store means immediate value for customers.

7. Initial iPad-specific apps will illustrate the advantage of iPad-specific device features (e.g., immersive experience, cinematic quality, etc.).

In April 2010, Apple released the iPad.

In the first 80 days of the launch, Apple sold three million units[2] and would eventually sell 14.8 million units in 2010. Because Apple had a well-developed business platform and a loyal and highly motivated business ecosystem, the company's executives learned a great deal about the use of the iPad and its users in the initial days following the launch. In the following months, more data poured in on its usage around the world.

In light of this data, Apple's initial active strategy playbook needed significant revision.

The iPad 2 would need to be revised for consumers and the iOS would need to made more enterprise-friendly, as 2010 data showed a significant trend in iPod adoption by corporations and, in particular, senior executives.

Apple executives had anticipated the value of the iPad but clearly underestimated demand, and failed to anticipate some new market segments. They learned that the iPad would necessitate changes in the MacOS and require other strategic moves as their products found use in industries new to Apple, such as health care.

These revisions, and the iterative nature of continuous active strategy, further boosted the iPad's command of the tablet market but also contributed to the meta-strategy allowing Apple a commanding view of new markets. And much of this can be traced back to the release of an SDK to developers. Meta-strategy, continuous active strategy and the playbook provided three levels of strategic adaptability and go-to market finesse.

Changing direction and having a powerful playbook is not the end of the story. Amazon, Apple and other elastic enterprises have two other weapons in their arsenal: strategic options portfolios and radical adjacency.

The Strategic Options Portfolio

A strategic option is an opportunity, but not an obligation, to take a course of action, usually based on a currently owned asset.

The asset could be simply an idea or it could be an existing product, a technological capability (e.g., factory, production process, information system), an invention or an investment in a company.

For each strategic option, the enterprise or executive team has the possibility of making a further investment of time, talent or capital.

All companies, everywhere, have some form of strategic options portfolio even if they don't actually express it. Sophisticated companies might have an extensive portfolio. But the chances are that even successful companies by traditional standards spend more time at the executive level managing existing brands, than they do developing their options.

It's one of the sad reflections of modern business practice that marginal improvements to brand performance preoccupy management.

One of the key features of an elastic enterprise is its ability to generate new strategic options in abundance, not least because radical adjacency moves are no longer a daunting prospect.

Looking at elastic enterprise in action you can see options proliferate, perhaps over-proliferate in some cases.

Google, in its early years, had one line of business: search.

Google invested heavily in its search platform and, through its innovative advertising business model, generated significant free cash flow and margins. As it continued to invest in the capacity of the search platform, it also began to notice new strategic options, for example, Google News, Google Apps and Google Maps.[3] The company began to develop a new meta-strategy, based in part on wishing to extend search opportunities but also something less articulated, a desire to be an agent of change.

In the case of News, Apps and Maps, Google decided to exercise the options and invest in developing new capabilities. That meant subject matter expertise, platform development, new hires, ecosystem development and new marketing strategies.

With each new capability that Google added to its business platform, it also generated new strategic options.

For example, Maps generated serious new options in location-specific and mobile business and probably convinced Google that it needed to go deeper into mobile, even to the point of owning a device company.

The investments drew more customers and generated more time spent with Google products, and therefore increased ad revenue.

On top of this, the extensions to the business platform drew new partners into the Google business ecosystem, not just through Android but also through its productivity apps platform, which in turn generated additional strategic options through more innovations.

Google Maps added an entirely new business ecosystem and also led to more users, new markets, new ad revenue and new licensing revenues by deploying Google Maps on other platforms (e.g., Apple iPhone, RIM) and products (e.g., automobiles). Google is now a major provider of destination booking information for high-end automobile owners.

Google Maps also spurred new acquisitions (e.g., ZipDash, Where2, Keyhole, Endoxon, ImageAmerica, Quiksee) to enhance its geospatial businesses. Google Maps' business platform allowed Google to enter local business markets to compete with the likes of Groupon.

The result: expansion of Google's strategic options portfolio.

Google is a great example of an elastic enterprise proliferating options, and of a management team unafraid to make radical adjacency moves. Compared to a traditional firm, every elastic enterprise is equally an option generation machine.

As these enterprises become better at creating real options,[4] they also advance their capacity to put a value on the entire strategic options portfolio. Ultimately the strategic options portfolio will help in calibrating the future value of the firm.

For evidence of this look at how Amazon was treated by analysts, even when its profits were lower than expected. Compare it with Salesforce.com which has a much less robust strategic options portfolio.

Salesforce.com's inability to grow its strategic options leaves it vulnerable to copycat competition in the CRM space.

By way of contrast, you hardly know which way Amazon might turn, next. The strategic options portfolio is multifaceted and dynamic, factors reflected in Amazon's share price.

The markets will punish companies with an under-developed strategic options portfolio, those that do not reflect strategic options in their acquisitions, and those without a demonstrable ability to implement adjacencies. Radical adjacency is a marker of elasticity.

Radical Adjacency

So far we have seen how meta-strategy, the active strategy playbook and the strategic options portfolio combine in a new kind of highly responsive continuous active strategy. But strategically, elastic enterprises have one other distinctive competitive advantage: radical adjacency.

Adjacencies have always been part of strategic thinking, but *radical adjacency* is strategic adjacency amplified. It introduces a whole new range of options into strategic options thinking and practice.

Traditional adjacencies are a way of extending an enterprise's core business into new geographies, new segments, new products or new processes.[5] M&A strategies often have adjacency objectives, but the success of many mergers and acquisition is limited.[6] With the exception of conglomerates, most adjacency moves are best when they stay close to the company's core products and, most importantly, core competencies.

In *radical adjacency*, the enterprise is able to move quickly to enter non-traditional markets that diverge significantly from a company's existing business and core competencies.

We need to understand how radical adjacency has suddenly become possible, and apparently straightforward.

How did the toughest move in business strategy become a repeatable process for enterprise innovators like Apple, Google and Amazon and indeed for less celebrated companies like USAA?

We can only really take an informed guess at how the five dynamics of the elastic enterprise enable radical adjacency.

Radical adjacency clearly benefits from the synergies of the business ecosystem, the business platform and universal connectors in the elastic enterprise.

The business ecosystem provides a means of enrolling new partners, new skills and tacit knowledge into the enterprise's playbook. That means elastic enterprises are able to draw in new talent and new knowledge very quickly.

This ability to forge relationships with entrepreneurial communities also allows elastic enterprises to harness a variant of open innovation. It's not strictly open innovation as we have understood it to date but it is a dynamic form of innovation that takes place in the interactions of many thousands of platform participants.

And as ecosystems tend to be customer facing, it means innovation is typically customer centric, allowing the elastic enterprise to quickly serve a variety of needs that are not being met.

These advantages certainly put an elastic enterprise in the position of being extremely adaptive.

In addition though the skills involved in creating and managing platforms seem to fit a company out for entering new markets.

The platform becomes a kind of Trojan horse. In itself it provides a uniquely powerful basis for competing in a new market—and the best example of this is Apple's ability to take on Nokia because it already had the iTunes platform.

The platform is a new core competency.

A robust business platform provides the infrastructure and tools as the elastic enterprise moves into unfamiliar markets.

The business platform also enables the elastic enterprise to flexibly add new apps, new means of production, new skills and new expertise as they move into new markets and new industries.

The platform also has the unique strength of allowing an elastic enterprise to serve many hundreds of micro-markets almost instantly. It provides the owner with a way of redefining the market landscape, based around the niche wants of customers. That too is a considerable competitive advantage.

Put another way, universal connectors, particularly APIs and Apps, mean that many new markets, in fact thousands of market niches, can be served with rapidly created, low friction, lightweight content and services, quickly building mass market adoption but with niche market levels of customer satisfaction.

Most importantly, the marketplace for APIs is expanding rapidly in all industries and global markets. Hence companies can expect a continuing stream of innovation and offering if they are have the ability to tune into a hyper-channel future.

The ability to enter rapidly and scale in a new industry, one that does not reflect the enterprise's prior core competency, is unprecedented.

Radical adjacency is often buttressed by more traditional strategic elements like M&A, R&D investments and innovation programs.

We suspect that acquisitions may be more accretive and more easily integrated when coupled with a robust business platform and a vibrant business ecosystem. Time will tell. Nonetheless, radical adjacency has amplified Apple's, Amazon's, Google's, USAA's, McLaren's and eBay's businesses:

- Amazon used its base platform in online book sales to move aggressively into other retail categories and then to develop an entire retail ecosystem of partners selling thousands of other retail product lines. Amazon continues with radical adjacency moves into IT services with its Cloud business and into Cloud-based electronic publishing with the Kindle platform.[7]

- Apple, long a single-product company, used the iPod and iPhone platforms to aggressively expand and diversify into the music, video, communications, software and publishing industries.

- USAA, long a user of the adjacency strategy in financial services through M&A and internal organic initiatives, employed radical adjacency as they moved into automotive buying and home buying services with the Auto Circle and Home Circle Cloud-based business platforms.

- McLaren, well known for its automotive racing prowess, is applying its real-time, race vehicle telemetry experience to develop new solutions and human telemetry apps for health care diagnostics and remote patient health monitoring.

- GE, with over 100 years of experience with adjacencies, has now established an entire business platform services division and is using elastic-type capabilities to support not only its aviation business, but also its medical equipment, energy, rail and leasing businesses. A recent review of GE press releases revealed an extensive use of the active playbook and strategic options portfolio throughout a wide range of its businesses, extracting additional value from existing adjacencies and entries into emerging industries and markets.[8]

As more companies establish elastic capabilities, we expect more companies to use radical adjacencies to leverage innovation, compete and generate growth.

The Future of the Elastic Enterprise

Many firms, particularly those that have invested effectively in information technology, have untapped potential to become elastic enterprises and develop active strategies, giving them unprecedented access to new options portfolios.

One of the areas we did not have space to touch on here but which is essential to the future of the elastic enterprise is the new social infrastructure provided by Facebook and Google +. While

Facebook has 800+ million users, Google has accumulated 90 million in just over half a year.

We already see businesses, especially in the start-up ecosystem, exploiting these social infrastructures at extraordinarily low cost by ramping up their marketing through social connections. Start-ups in particular are using Facebook as their main business platform.

That practice will further reduce business frictions and create more symmetry between the enterprise and customers, no doubt once again morphing how we create wealth together.

The keystone change is instantaneous global interconnectedness, which even some of our elastic enterprises have yet to master.

The Five Dynamics discussed in Chapters 3 and 4 are the basis of enterprise elasticity.

The six behaviors that sapient leaders leverage are a high-level expression of the capabilities of the elastic enterprise. These leaders drive their enterprises to greater innovation and growth.

When combined with a continuous active strategy, the new strategic options portfolio and radical adjacency, the elastic enterprise becomes a highly disruptive competitor.

As we look to the future, we see elastic enterprises well positioned to exploit powerful megatrends in mobile technologies, further developments with the Cloud and new consumer and employee norms in social networking.

The five dynamics of the elastic enterprise, and more specifically, business platforms, business ecosystems and universal connectors, leverage vast inputs from employees, partners, customers and, upcoming, digital sensors and devices.

The greatest challenge for elastic enterprises, as with all enterprises, will be leadership and decision-making.

The ability of the elastic enterprise to move and scale quickly can become a major liability without sapient leadership. Several recent examples show how companies with promising business platforms and promising business ecosystems fail to capitalize on their advantages. Yahoo, Netflix, AOL and RIM come to mind.

Elastic enterprises will also need to watch security threats closely as digital warfare and hacker networks set their sights on digital assets. And they may begin to receive significant regulatory scrutiny given their competitive power and ability to drive radical adjacencies.

Of course regulatory intervention will depend on the degree that other firms can begin to adopt approaches used by the elastic enterprise and mount competitive counter measures of their own. In our opinion, we are just beginning to see the power of elastic enterprises to transform markets and industries.

At the same time, elastic enterprises must be mindful of any hint of monopolistic practices and the hubris that tends to accompany overwhelming market power.

Monopolies, by definition, are overly restrictive with respect to trade and competition. We think that while monopolistic and other zero sum practices might be attractive in the short run, they should be avoided. Such practices will ultimately strangle an elastic enterprise because closed business ecosystems ultimately atrophy without new members and are ultimately toxic to invention, transformation and growth.

We're also watching "traditional companies" that have some of the elements and have been making some promising moves on their journey to elasticity. For example,

- Boeing could build further upon its sophistical design and manufacturing ecosystem and related business platforms; it already has a tradition of acquisitive and organic adjacency moves.

- Wal-Mart's recent media and social acquisitions of VUDU, Kosmix, OneRiot, and Small Society could significantly enhance its closed, but massive global logistics platform and vendor business ecosystem and add significant elasticity to its business.

- Caterpillar is a global innovator in the use of information technology and has recently created industry standards for universal connectors like its API for remote electronic control of heavy industrial equipment.[9] Its business platforms and business ecosystems along with partnerships with companies like Trimble Navigation show important moves to elasticity.[10]

- Deere & Company, a long-time investor in advanced information technology and designer of integrated agricultural equipment and system products, is positioned with elastic capabilities. Its recent John Deere FarmSight offering combines a business platform, a business ecosystem of dealers and suppliers, advanced telemetry, and big data to support farm managers.[11]

- IBM continues to expand its social and big data businesses, to amass business platform components and is rapidly building global business ecosystems in energy, government, buildings and education, and has significant experience from its involvement in the Linux business ecosystem and related platforms.

- Cisco, a long-time fan of portals and expert communities, understands the power of networks and has the potential to bring its assets together to form an elastic enterprise, especially with its investments in API management experts Mashery.

Nonetheless, existing elastic enterprises have a current advantage. There is still much to learn about the elastic enterprise. We have merely scratched the surface. As we have seen, in the hands of inspired and uniquely talented sapient leaders like the late Steve Jobs, Jeff Bezos or Larry Page, even the most grizzled competitor must take note. Given these advantages, the elastic enterprise is truly a living and formative manifesto for business revolution.

THE MAIN POINTS REVIEWED:

Strategy is changing. Episodic strategy setting is out. Continuous strategy setting is necessary but not sufficient. Strategy has to be actively managed.

In order to do continuous active strategy management enterprises need to build a powerful strategic options portfolio, including products and opportunities they might never use. To do continuous strategy you have to be at the ready and have an active strategy playbook

All this is dependent on having the right flows of data and those come from a strong business platform and a vibrant ecosystem as well as from formal external data sources.

With these pieces in place, and the five dynamics of the elastic enterprise, successful companies are finding they can execute the most difficult of all business strategies—radical adjacency.

To see how close you are to a continuous active strategy ask:

1. How close is our strategy setting to a continuous process? How would we move to a continuous active strategy process?
2. Do we know how capable we are at maintaining confidentiality across a broad range of core strategic options?
3. How many of our acquisitions have opened up new market opportunities?
4. What is our track record with M&A? With organic business initiatives?
5. How are we positioned to take advantage of rapidly developing economies?
6. Where do we get our key data? Do we get intelligence from our partnerships?
7. What data do we create? Do our products and services generate data during use? If so what kind of data?

8. What dashboards might we use to aggregate and distribute data in real time?

9. What is our confidence level that the right data gets to the right decision makers at the right time?

10. Does our data impel action?

11. Do we own real data interpretation skills, not just data management skills?

12. If a country like France suddenly defaulted on its debt, how would it affect our suppliers?

13. How many times recently have we been open to product ideas from small companies?

14. How are our strategic options generated? Are they systematically cataloged and reviewed. By whom?

15. What products do we have ready to launch if the market looked right tomorrow?

16. How would you rate your company's ability to use outsiders to independently augment our products and services?

17. How quickly do our venture teams or innovation departments take us into new markets?

---

[1] Steve Jobs in a public letter to the Apple Development Community announces plans for an SDK for the iPhone, "Third Party Applications on the iPhone," *Apple Hot News*, August 17, 2007.

[2] "Apple Sells Three Million iPads in 80 Days," http://www.apple.com/pr/library/2010/06/22Apple-Sells-Three-Million-iPads-in-80-Days.html, *Apple Press Info*, Apple Inc., June 22, 2010.

[3] At the time, Google encouraged, some might say mandated, that each employee dedicate 20 percent of his or her paid time to innovate (e.g., one day per week).

[4] For a summary overview of real options, see "Real Options Valuation," Wikipedia. For a more detailed examination of real options and their use in enterprises, see Johnathan Mun, Real Options Analysis: Tools and Techniques for Valuing Strategic Investment and Decisions, 2nd Edition, New Jersey: John Wiley & Sons, Inc., 2006. For an illustrative case study, see Tom Arnold and Richard

L. Shockley, Jr., "Value Creation at Anheuser-Busch: A Real Options Example," http://www.ucm.es/info/jmas/doctor/beer.pdf.

[5] For a discussion of the role of adjacencies in relationship to core business, see Chris Zook and James Allen, *Profit from the Core: Growth Strategy in an Era of Turbulence, Updated Edition*, Bain & Company, Inc., 2010.

[6] For further discussion of the problems with traditional approaches to adjacency and why this must and can change, see Haydn Shaughnessy, "Radical Adjacency Comes of Age with HP's Autonomy Buy, Google and Motorola," http://www.forbes.com/sites/haydnshaughnessy/2011/08/23/hps-autonomy-buy-google-and-motorola/, *Forbes*, August 23, 2011. See also Haydn Shaughnessy, "The Rise of Radical Adjacency," http://www.forbes.com/sites/haydnshaughnessy/2011/07/14/the-rise-of-radical-adjacency/, *Forbes*, July 14, 2011.

[7] More recently, Amazon used its expertise in adjacency to move into the IT services industry as a major player in Cloud services. That business contributes over $600 million to Amazon's top line according to UBS and is expected to reach the $1 billion mark by 2013. Similarly, Amazon's aggressive moves into the device business with its Kindle electronic publishing product and now its Fire Tablet device is a radical adjacency move into sourced manufacturing, with the added adjacency of becoming a publishing house in 2011.

[8] www.ge.com, search results from "platform services," December 16, 2011.

[9] The AEMP Telematics Data Standard V1.1 was made official on October 1, 2010, http://www.aemp.org/resources/Telematics_Standards.pdf. See also http://www.oemoffhighway.com/article/10181908/ telematics-linking-the-future-now and http://www.constructionequipment.com/article/aemp-oems- advance-industry-telematics-standard for further commentary on the open-API standard.

[10] Source: http://www.trimble.com/news/faq.shtml, Virtual Site FAQ, Caterpillar Joint Venture Announcement

[11] Source: http://www.deere.com/en_US/CCE_promo/farmsight/index.html

ACKNOWLEDGEMENTS

It takes a community to build a book and we have had the opportunity to work with an insightful group of bright and influential folks over the years. All have influenced our thinking and work, given us encouragement and as a consequence deserve mention and thanks.

They include Paul Artiuch, Russ Aebig, Espen Andersen, Dave Banks, Tim Bevins, Joan Bigham, Jen Bigora, Erik Britt-Webb, Bob Buday, Frank Capek, Laura Carrillo, Tom Casey, James Cash, James Champy, Richard Chavez, Lisa Chen, Ron Christman, Peter Cochrane, Ian Da Silva, Jeff DeChambeau, Tony Dirumaldo, Mike Dover, Debra Dunkle, Walter DuLaney, Ruth Dunleavey, Stephanne Ebsen, Tammy Erickson, Jos Echelpoels, Doffie Farrar, Mark Fling, Maryantonett Flumian, Michael Glavich, James Glover, Steve Guengerich, Vijay Gurbaxani, Denis Hancock, Naumi Haque, Dan Herman, Deb Harrity, Brian Janz, Tom Kelly, John L. King, Kenneth Kraemer, David Kruzner, Dave Laveman, Al Leveckis, Alan Majer, Brian Majierski, Ruth Malone, Ed Mello, Vaughan Merlyn, Robert Morison, Tom Nickles, Michael O'Farrell, Dennis O'Malley, Steve Papermaster, Honorio Padron, Keri Pearlson, Walter Popper, Mark Rennella, Gary Roberts, Ed Roche, Bruce Rogow, Judy Rosen, Christine Sanger, Margaret Schweer, Andrew Shimberg, Don Tapscott, Kary Taylor, Colby Thames, David Trafford, Albert Travis, Alladi Venkatesh, Jay Wagman, James Wetherbe, Anthony Williams, Dylan Williams, and Roy Youngman.

We solicited comments on earlier versions on the web and would like to extend our appreciation and gratitude to the individuals that reviewed early chapters and provided their valuable comments. On the development of APIs we have benefited from conversations with Oren Michels, CEO, and Randi Barshack, VP marketing at Mashery Inc. We are grateful to Jay M. Williams, Vice President of Engineering for Cloud Commons and Cloud Ecosystem at CA

Technologies and Internet pioneer, who significantly advanced our understanding of the Cloud.

Writing anything of this length requires an understanding family. Haydn would like to thank his wife Roos who has maintained order with our children while I type away and she looked after them while I travelled. Each of them deserves a medal for putting up with me and my absences, and my absent mindedness. On the professional front in addition to the people who have inspired Nick and I, I would also like to thank the many people who write to me at Forbes. com usually to say they appreciate my writing and my point of view. I guarantee you will get more of it! Your willingness to reach out tells me I'm getting something right and I appreciate it deeply.

Nick would like to thank his wife Martha who supports him in his long hours in the office and again when he surfaces. And I want to thank my two sons, Paul and Joe, who could not make a father more proud. They are always supportive, understanding, and I thank them for their contribution to this endeavor. I owe a debt of gratitude to my sister-in-law, Mary Sue Schulte, an artist and author, for her recommendations and assistance on publishing e-books. And last but not least to my sister, brother-in-law, niece and nephew, Lori, Glenn, Susan and Thomas.

We deeply appreciate our community, our colleagues and our friends. They make life meaningful and worthwhile. Nonetheless, despite all the assistance and encouragement, we take full responsibility for the content of this book including any errors and omissions.

ABOUT THE AUTHORS

Nicholas Vitalari

Nicholas Vitalari is renowned for his work in re-integrating business strategy and technology. He has also been a business founder, academic and business leader. He was previously a senior executive at Index, CSC, and was co-founder, EVP, and Director of The Concours Group, which grew from a start-up to $50 million in revenues in three years. Nick was a professor of management at UC Irvine before going into business. He is the author of three prior books and numerous articles in academic journals, books, and the professional press. His work has been featured in The Wall Street Journal, The Los Angeles Times, and Psychology Today as well as on radio and television.

Haydn Shaughnessy

Haydn Shaughnessy is a writer and commentator on the evolution of social business and the digital transformation of society. His work embraces semantic analysis of emerging patterns of thought and behavior. He has worked as a visiting fellow at nGenera Insight, a senior research associate of the European Institute for the Media, and the Centre for Employment Research as well as a program manager for advanced communications projects at the European Union. He writes the Re:Thinking Innovation column at Forbes.com and has written on design and innovation for the Irish Times. He has written for GigaOm, The Wall St Journal, The Times, Radio Times, and many other outlets.

CPSIA information can be obtained at www.ICGtesting.com
Printed in the USA
BVOW070915241212

309011BV00002B/6/P

9 781938 135347